D1531698

VIRGINIA

By Allan Carpenter

Illustrations by Roger Herrington

ℂℙ CHILDRENS PRESS, CHICAGO

Consultant

Ray Hiner, Jr., Supervisor of History,
Richmond Public Schools

For their advice, counsel and gracious help, the author thanks:

Mills E. Godwin, Jr., Governor
Ray Hiner, Jr., Supervisor of History, Richmond Public Schools
Division of Industrial Development and Planning
Department of Conservation and Economic Development
Department of Highways
Department of Agriculture and Immigration
Virginia State Chamber of Commerce
Evanston, Illinois, Public Library
Tom Balow

Library of Congress Catalog Card Number: 67–20093

Copyright©, 1967, Childrens Press, Inc.
All rights reserved. Printed in the U.S.A.
Published simultaneously in Canada

2 3 4 5 6 7 8 9 10 11 12 13 14 15 16 17 18 19 20 21 22 23 24 25   R 75 74 73 72 71 70 69 68

Contents

A True Story to Set the Scene

Colonel George Washington was hurrying to Williamsburg in May, 1758. Crossing the Pamunkey River he met Colonel Richard Chamberlayne, who invited him to dinner at his home, Poplar Grove. Washington assured him that the dispatches he was carrying would not permit him to linger even for a moment. Then Colonel Chamberlayne made a statement that immediately attracted the young man soon to be a hero of the French and Indian Wars. If Washington stayed for dinner, Colonel Chamberlayne promised, he would meet "the prettiest and richest widow in Virginia."

Washington quickly gave in; he agreed to "dine—only dine;" by "borrowing of the night" he might reach Williamsburg the next morning.

The story of George Washington and his pretty dinner partner is one of the many stories of the enchantment of Virginia. And it has in it many of the things which are so typical of the history of the Old Dominion—famous and wealthy people, handsome plantations, courtly hospitality and romance.

While his faithful servant Bishop held his master's dashing horse, Washington lingered inside, detained by the charms of the pretty widow, Martha Dandridge Custis, until finally Colonel Chamberlayne said that no guest of his left his home at such a late hour, and Washington stayed the night.

On other trips he visited with Martha Custis at her splendid estate, called the White House. Only two months after their first meeting, Colonel Washington was writing "to one whose life is now inseparable from mine. Since that happy hour when we made our pledges to each other, my thoughts have been continually going to you as to another self."

When the French and Indian War had diminished, George Washington and Martha Custis were married in January, 1759. Strangely the exact date and place are unknown, although it probably was on January 6 at the bride's White House estate.

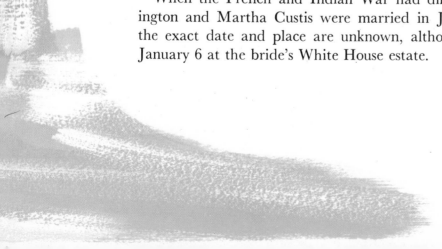

Many years later Martha's grandson spoke to a servant of his grandmother who had reached a hundred years of age, "And so you remember when Colonel Washington came a courting of your mistress?"

"Ay, master, that I do, great times, sir, great times! . . ." Of Washington the ancient servant said, "Never the likes of him . . . so tall, so straight and then he sat a horse and rode with such an air! Ah, sir; he was like no one else! Many of the grandest gentlemen in their gold lace were at the wedding, but none looked like the man himself!"

A rare old account describes the bride's wedding dress: "A white satin quilt, over which a heavy white silk, interwoven with threads of silver, was looped back with white satin ribbons, richly brocaded in a leaf pattern. Her bodice was of plain satin, and the brocade was fastened on the bust with a stiff butterfly bow of the ribbon. Delicate lace finished the low, square neck. There were close elbow sleeves revealing a puff and frill of lace. Strings of pearls were woven in and out of her powdered hair. Her high-heeled slippers were of white satin, with brilliant buckles."

The couple spent their honeymoon in Williamsburg while the groom took his place in the House of Burgesses and the bride closed her town house at Williamsburg.

Paul Wilstach in *Mount Vernon* writes: "As soon as the Burgesses rose, the Colonel and his bride and her two children with their attendants and light luggage, flew across the country in their own coach, behind four galloping thoroughbreds, whips cracking and dust clouds rolling, faster and faster, but not so fast as their eagerness to reach the house of his promise and her hope. . . ." Then at last, "over the highlands past the old parish church, down Michael Reagen's hill, through another valley with two or three branches to ford, up the long hill at the west end of Colonel Fairfax's lands, and, as the road descends again, with the Potomac in sight at the right, an interminable valley on the left, its long reach lost in the purple haze of the distant hills, and before them the glistening white villa on the high horizon three miles to the east, they came on to their own domain. They were home . . ." to start a new life at Mount Vernon.

When Washington left his beloved estate again sixteen years later, he began a course which would establish a new country which has become one of the greatest in the family of nations.

Honor to the Virgin Queen

In 1497 explorer John Cabot made an extended voyage along the northern shoreline of North America. Years later, because of this exploration, eager ministers of Queen Elizabeth I claimed for Her Majesty all the vast region north of the lands claimed by the Spanish. In honor of the Virgin Queen they named the entire region Virginia.

At one time this huge empire included (at least on paper) most of what we now call conterminous United States. Although the Virginia of the present has shrunk from this once tremendous area, today's Virginia can still look back proudly to being the "Mother of the States."

Virginia Today

Virginia today covers 40,815 square miles, including 977 square miles of inland water surface. Much of this water area is made up of the fat fingers of water (called estuaries) which reach far inland from the sea. Greatest of these, of course, is Chesapeake Bay. Others of these great "drowned river valleys" are the estuaries of the James, York, and Rappahannock rivers. The estuary of the Potomac River is not within the boundaries of Virginia, since the state boundary is set at the Potomac waterline as far north as the tides flow.

These great estuaries cut the mainland into three parallel peninsulas. Across Chesapeake Bay is another peninsula—Virginia's portion of the Delmarva Peninsula (shared by Delaware, Maryland and Virginia). The Virginia portion is itself a smaller peninsula jutting off from the larger one.

Virginia is drained by nine major rivers: Potomac, Rappahannock, York, James, Chowan, Roanoke, New (in spite of its name one of the oldest on the continent), Tennessee and Big Sandy. The last three flow to the north and west and eventually reach the Mississippi; for that reason they are called Virginia's "Western Waters."

Three great river systems, Rappahannock, York and James, flow almost their entire courses within the state. The James cuts a four-mile opening through the Blue Ridge Mountains in order to empty into Chesapeake Bay instead of the Ohio River system. The Roanoke River flows across

State Seal

MARYLAND

Winchester
Bull Run Mts.
Front Royal
Falls Church
Luray Cavern
Arlington
Shenandoah River Valley
Alexandria
WEST VIRGINIA
Manassas
Shenandoah
Shenandoah Tower
Nat'l. Park
Shenandoah
Fredericksburg
Shenandoah
Nat'l. Park
Spotsylvania
George Washington
Birthplace Nat'l.
Mem.
Staunton
Monticello
Waynesboro
Charlottesville
Chincoteague
MOUNTAINS
PLATEAU
Lexington
Potomac River
KENTUCKY
VALLEY
RIDGE
RICHMOND
COASTAL
PLAIN
Rappahannock River
WEST VIRGINIA
Natural Bridge
Lynchburg
York River
Yorktown
APPALACHIAN
GREAT
Roanoke
Appomattox River
Jamestown
Big Stone Ridge
BLUE
Appomattox
Petersburg
Colonial Nat'l
Hist. Park
Williamsburg
Walker Mtn.
Martinsville
PIEDMONT
Danville
Roanoke River
John H. Kerr Res.
Newport News
Hampton Roads
Iron Mts.
Portsmouth
Norfolk
Bristol
Mt. Rogers
Dismal Swamp
Suffolk
False Cape
TENNESSEE
NORTH CAROLINA

John Tyler
Tenth President of the U.S.; 1841-1845

James Madison
Fourth President of the U.S.; 1809-1817

William Henry Harrison
Ninth President of the U.S.; 1841; died after only 31 days in office

Woodrow Wilson
Twenty-eighth President of the U.S.; 1913-1921

Zachary Taylor
Twelfth President of the U.S.; 1849-1850

Thomas Jefferson
Third President of the U.S.; 1801-1809

George Washington
First President of the U.S.; 1789-1797

James Monroe
Fifth President of the U.S.; 1817-1825

General Robert E. Lee
Most outstanding military leader of the Confederacy

State Bird: Cardinal

State Flower: Flowering Dogwood

Virginia for 240 miles before entering North Carolina. Other large Virginia rivers are the Clinch, Holston and Powell.

The "portals" of Chesapeake Bay consist of Cape Charles on the north and Cape Henry on the south. Where the waters of the Nansemond, James and Elizabeth rivers empty into Chesapeake Bay, one of the world's finest natural harbors—Hampton Roads—has been formed. This is just a part of the huge 3,315-mile tidal shoreline of Virginia.

Major lakes are all man-made. They include Smith Mountain Lake, Philpott Reservoir, Claytor Lake, Lessville Lake and parts of Buggs Island Lake and Lake Gaston. These latter two are shared with North Carolina. Many other smaller reservoirs dot the state.

Virginia's neighbor states are Maryland, West Virginia, Kentucky, Tennessee and North Carolina. Geographers divide Virginia into five main areas known as physiographic provinces—Coastal Plain, Piedmont, Blue Ridge, Valley and Ridge, and Appalachian Plateau.

Between the Coastal Plain and the Piedmont is the Fall Line. The major rivers can be navigated to this line. The Blue Ridge is the highest section of the state—a kind of craggy backbone. The western and northern portions of the state are seamed and creased with other rows of parallel mountain systems and valleys. One of America's most famous valleys—a name known to almost everyone through song and story—is the Shenandoah Valley. The tallest peak in Virginia is Mount Rogers, in the extreme southwest, rising to 5,729 feet.

Where Virginia's westward-aimed "dart" comes to its sharp point is White Top Mountain; there the three states of Kentucky, Virginia and Tennessee come together at famed Cumberland Gap. It is interesting to note that Cumberland Gap is 25 miles farther west than Detroit, making part of Virginia "midwestern."

In the Distant Past

Many times, in a past too far distant even to imagine, much of what is now Virginia west of the Blue Ridge was flooded by ancient seas. Then the shrinking of the earth squeezed enormous folds of the rocky layers of the earth into the air, forming the ancestors of today's Appalachian Mountains.

13

Over unbelievable ages of time, wind and water wore these great ranges almost level. They were raised up again, eroded down, and raised a third time. The present Appalachians, including the Blue Ridge, Shenandoah and Allegheny mountains, are probably 800,000,000 years old, among the oldest mountains on the earth's surface. If the earth lasts long enough, they probably will be worn down once more to the level of the land around them.

Dinosaur footprints of Loudoun County, whales' teeth, portions of ancient elephants and the fossil plants of Virginia coal fields are among the traces left of the living things of the ancient past.

Climate

Even in midsummer Virginia temperatures are moderate, and cool in the mountains. In midwinter, heavy or long-lying snow is rare. Precipitation, averaging 45 inches per year, is spread throughout the months. Spring comes early and stays late. By late April gardens are magnificent. Even before that, the long wild flower parade has begun. Fall is equally long and delightful. In the mountains, autumn turns the great hardwood forests into a breathtaking kaleidoscope of color. In Virginia's tidewater, the best of summer lingers late, with ocean swimming possible generally well into October.

Collecting Your Thoughts

A glance at the map will indicate that much of Virginia is dominated by two or three types of natural features. What would you say these are?

Of "Grave and Majesticall Countenance"

Just before the coming of the first settlers to the region, the most distinctive and unusual Indian civilization of what is now the United States had its headquarters in the area that later became the state of Virginia.

The only truly royal or kingly personage who ever ruled an Indian kingdom in this country was the great king Wahunsonacock, or Powhatan as the English called him. His cunning in war and diplomacy had enabled him to weld a confederacy of 30 separate kingdoms under his autocratic rule. The confederacy included, some say, as many as 161 villages, with an army of 2,400 trained warriors. These people were of the Algonquin language stock, one of the three main language groups in what is now Virginia.

The others were the tribes of Sioux stock, living generally in what is now north central Virginia, and the Iroquois tribes. Some of the Sioux tribes were grouped into what is known as the Monacan Confederacy. Most of the Iroquois tribes did not make permanent homes in present Virginia, but they tried to extend the authority of the Iroquois Confederacy ever farther southward. The Rickohockan group and other Cherokee-related groups are usually identified with the Iroquois, and they lived in the mountain regions of the present state.

King Powhatan ruled from 36 different tribal capitals, in each of which he had a royal house. The empire of Powhatan was subdivided into parts, each ruled by a civil leader known as a *sachem* and a war leader (*werowance*). Leaders were advised by the priests and a group of leaders known as the tribal council. Each division had its capital, or seat of government.

When Captain John Smith first visited the principal Indian capital of Werowocomoco, he found the "Emperor proudly lying upon a Bedstead a foote high, upon tenn or twelve mattes, richly hung with manie Chaynes of great Pearles about his necke, and covered with great Covering of *Rahaughcums*. At (his) head sat a woman, at his feete another; on each side sitting upon a Matte uppon the ground, were raunged his chiefe men on each side the fire, tenne in a ranke, and behinde them as many yong women, each (with) a great Chaine of white Beades over their shoulders, their heades painted in redde: and (Powhatan) with such a grave Majesticall countenance, as drave me into admiration to see such state in a naked Salvage."

The villages, houses, clothing, crafts, hunting, agriculture and religion of the Indians in what is now Virginia were generally similar to those of other eastern regions. One of the more interesting customs was the "sweating house," heated with red-hot stones. It resembled the Finnish sauna, growing popular in modern America.

Another strange custom was the manner of burial of the chiefs. The leader's body was disemboweled upon his death and stuffed with sand, wrapped and laid in the temple, where it dried, mummy-like.

There were so many small tribes and their exact locations were so uncertain that space does not permit to describe them here, although many of the individual groups and their leaders are mentioned later in this volume.

Comparatively little is known about the people who lived in Virginia before historic times and on into the distant ages of prehistoric times. Some of their mounds, such as Hayes Creek, and other remains, like the stone implement quarries near New Hampden, have been examined, and many relics of early periods are exhibited in a somewhat scattered way in museums throughout the state. An Indian mound near Ruckersville was described by Thomas Jefferson in his *Notes on Virginia*.

A Town for James the King

Historians draw a blank on the first European discoverer of what is now Virginia. Some of the early explorers of America certainly passed by, and may have set foot on the present state. Both the English and Spanish laid claim to the region, and the Spanish Jesuit missionaries had set up a mission on the banks of Aquia Creek in the Potomac region as early as the 1580's. However, the missionaries were massacred by the Indians. The Indians long remembered the violent deeds of the soldiers sent north by the Spaniards to avenge the killing of their religious men.

In 1606 King James I of England chartered two companies, the London Company to colonize southern Virginia (probably everything south of Chesapeake Bay) and the Plymouth Company to colonize northern Virginia (roughly everything to the north of Chesapeake Bay).

On April 26, 1607, three little ships, the flagship *Susan Constant,* with the *Discovery* and *Godspeed,* came ashore at what is now Virginia Beach and their people set up a cross to show their thankfulness at arriving in the New World. They named the place where they landed Cape Henry and the opposite cape of this huge mouth of the ocean Cape Charles to honor the king's sons. Here they opened the sealed instructions which they had carried across the ocean, to find just what the London Company required them to do in their new land.

They moved slowly up the great estuary, and on the evening of May 14, 1607, the little ships were according to their own account "moored to the trees in 6 fathoms of water," off an island in the river. That night, as a forecast of difficulties in the future, the Indians came "creeping upon all foure from the Hills, like Beares, with their Bowes in their mouthes."

The next morning the very first Virginians, 105 in number, went ashore and "set to work about the fortification." Inside the tiny fort they began a chapel, some huts with thatched roofs and a storehouse. In honor of the king, they named the little settlement James Town, later Jamestown.

They could not have known it, but this was to become the first permanent English settlement in America.

When the colonists landed, one of the men was in chains for some minor cause. This was John Smith. However, when the colonists opened their sealed orders it was found that Smith was to be one of the members of the governing council, so Smith was freed. Gradually Smith became the acknowledged leader.

A large number of the colonists considered themselves "gentlemen" and too dignified for ordinary labor. There was much bickering and arguing over what ought to be done. Smith persuaded a number of them that they had to work; when blisters appeared on their hands they began to swear; at this point Smith threatened to pour pitchers of cold water down their sleeves if they continued their swearing.

John Smith was captured by Indians in 1607 and finally taken to Powhatan's capital of Werowocomoco. This was the scene of one of the world's most famous stories. No one can say whether or not the story is true. Powhatan is said to have ordered Smith beheaded; just before the executioner brought his hatchet down, a beautiful young Indian girl is supposed to have thrown her body over Smith to protect him and save his life. This, of course, was the glamorous thirteen-year-old Princess Pocahontas, daughter of Powhatan. It is probably true that she saved Smith from death even if not in quite such a romantic manner.

Not long after, Smith persuaded Powhatan to trade supplies much needed by the colonists for some glass beads and other trinkets. King James was so impressed by the description of Powhatan's power that he ordered the colonists to crown him.

When Smith and the others went to Werowocomoco, the great Indian king was away, so the women put on a dance to entertain the visitors, as Smith described it: "Thirtie young women came . . . out of the woods . . . their bodies all painted . . . with most hellish shouts and cryes, rushing from among the trees, cast themselves in a ring about the fire, singing and dauncing with most excellent ill varietie. . . ."

Powhatan refused to go to Jamestown, so the colonists held the ceremony of coronation in his own capital. Later, when the colonists needed more supplies, the king was not satisfied with glass beads. He demanded and got a European-type house. This house remained standing until 1915 and then was carefully restored.

The teen-aged Pocahontas often visited Jamestown, where she flitted about merrily and entertained the settlers by turning cartwheels around the walls of the stockade. She was fascinated by Captain Smith, and apparently fell madly in love with him, but he ignored her.

In October of 1609 Captain John Smith returned to England for medical treatment of severe injuries. The London Company had never sent enough supplies for the colony's needs, and most of the settlers sent by the company did not know how to do useful work. Smith wrote a letter, known as his "rude letter," to the company, saying, "When you send againe I entreat you rather send but thirty Carpenters, husbandmen, gardiners, fishermen, blacksmiths, masons and diggers up of trees, roots, well provided; than a thousand of such as we have: for except wee be able both to lodge them and feed them, the most will consume with want of necessaries before they can be made good for anything."

The winter of 1609-1610 became known as the "starving time." Food was almost gone; the region was unhealthy and many took sick. When the winter started, the colony numbered 500; by May only 65 miserable survivors were left. They abandoned Jamestown and started for England. At Mulberry Island, only 14 miles away, they met Lord De la Warr, who had come from England with supplies and new settlers. Encouraged by this, the survivors turned back.

Progress

In 1614 John Rolfe became the "savior of the colony." He promoted the growing of tobacco, which proved to be a successful crop, much in demand in England. He also married Princess Pocahontas, who had been brought to Jamestown as a hostage. Danger from the Indians had been increasing up until this time, but after the marriage, Rolfe's father-in-law, Powhatan, kept his people generally in line until his death probably in 1616. Rolfe wrote that he married the princess not for love but "for the honour of our countrie."

By 1619 it appeared the colony might succeed. It was divided into 11 regularly established plantations, including several settlements such as Henricopolis (or Henricus). Henry Hamor, colonial secretary, wrote a revealing description of Henricus: "There is in this town three streets, of well framed houses, a handsome church, and the foundation of a more stately one laid of brick, in length an hundred foote, and fifty foote wide, beside store houses, watch houses, and such like; there are also, as ornaments belonging to this town, upon the verge of this river, five faire blockhouses, or commanders, wherein live the honnestes sort of peoples, as in farmes in England, and there keep continuall centinell for the townes security. . . ."

In 1619 occurred one of the significant events of our country's history. An election was held "by ye Ballot boxe," to choose two representatives from each of the 11 plantations of the colony to form a "House of Burgess." This became the first democratically elected legislative body in the New World. As the Virginia legislature today, it has now become the oldest continuously operating legislative body in the Western Hemisphere.

Also in 1619 the colony was organized into four "incorporations" or major divisions resembling the later counties.

Another event of 1619 was the arrival of the first Negroes, from a Dutch ship. These, however, were not to be slaves but were allowed to come in as indentured servants, who would be free after a time of service.

A Period of Trouble

After the death of Powhatan, Indian rule in the region was taken over by King Opechancanough. He pretended friendship with the settlers, but laid careful plans to drive them from the country. Opechancanough instructed his followers to attack at precisely the same hour on March 22, 1622, along a 140-mile front covering most of the settled area of the colony.

In this "deadly stroake" 347 colonists lost their lives. The Indian plan might have succeeded completely, but Jamestown was saved by Chanco, a converted Indian youth, who warned the people of the coming attack.

Many years passed before Virginia was able to recover from this massacre. Plans for setting up schools and universities to convert and educate the Indians were abandoned. A six-mile-long palisade was built across the peninsula as protection against Indian attack.

The last great Indian uprising in eastern Virginia came in 1644. Aged Opechancanough made a final desperate effort but was put down. Two years later the king was captured by a force under Governor William Berkeley and carried wounded on a stretcher to Jamestown. There he was shot by a soldier who was supposed to guard him. The mightiest Indian empire north of Mexico had been made powerless.

Seeds of Freedom

By this time Virginia was ruled as a royal colony. The London Company charter had been revoked in 1624. However, there was a growing independence in the colony. The king had recognized the House of Burgesses in 1628, and as early as 1635 the House of Burgesses had been able to cause the removal of one royal governor.

Forty years later there was an even more important revolt against royal government. Sir William Berkeley had been away from the governorship for some years when he was selected again in 1660 by the Burgesses. Over the years, his rule became more powerful and less interested in the people.

In 1674 Nathaniel Bacon began to rally the people against the governor, who refused to defend the western frontiers against Indian attack. More and more followers joined him. Although Berkeley called him "the greatest rebel that ever was in Virginia," he was forced to pardon him. Later Bacon virtually took over the government, and Berkeley fled to the eastern shore.

However, he returned to Jamestown, and Bacon and his followers attacked the town and set it on fire. Then Bacon wrote what has come to be known as "America's first declaration of independence." In a proclamation Bacon declared that if the king of England upheld Berkeley, the people of Virginia would have to fight for their liberties or leave the colony. He started off on a trip around Virginia to persuade people to stand firm, but he died of a fever on the trip.

Berkeley hanged twenty of Bacon's leaders without trial and took over the property of many others. On hearing of this, the king wrote, "That old fool has hanged more men in that naked country than I have done here for the murder of my father."

However, Bacon's stirring message had aroused Virginians so much that a hundred years later they were perhaps better prepared to declare their independence than any other group.

The years that followed were a period of exploration, with the frontier pushing westward, and of growth and development. It was a time of pirates and finally the destruction of most of them, of authorizing ports, of treaties with the Indians, and of the moving of the capital. In 1699 Williamsburg, named in honor of King William III, was made the capital.

Plantation Life

In 1716 pleasure-loving Governor Alexander Spotswood led a famous expedition to the west, looking for a new pass over the mountains. Carrying a large supply of almost every wine and liquor known, the governor and his merry party drank toasts on practically every occasion. When the merry explorers returned, the governor had miniature golden horseshoes made and covered with jewels; he gave each member of his party one of these emblems, and the men became known as "Knights of the Golden Horseshoe."

By the time Governor Spotswood retired in 1722, he had acquired 85,000 acres of land "among ye little mountains" and lived like a king on his estate, decorated with terraced gardens and a marble fountain. In his elegant drawing rooms, a "brace of tame deer ran familiarly through the house." As governor, he had little concern about entertaining 400 for dinner, even on short notice.

Governor Spotswood was not alone in his luxurious living. In Virginia the plantation system reached its peak of wealth, cultivated manners and elegant living. Each plantation was almost like a self-sufficient little world to itself, presided over by the owners, many of whom behaved like minor rulers.

Thomas Lord Fairfax inherited from his mother the proprietary of Northern Neck, a vast estate of 5,000,000 acres, including all the land between the Rappahannock and Potomac rivers. This was the largest estate in Virginia, but there were others almost as big.

As early as 1649 a writer had described Denbigh Plantation owned by Samuel Mathews: "He . . . sowes yearly a store of Hemp and Flax, and causes it to be spun; he keeps Weavers and hath a Tan-house, causes

Leather to be dressed, hath eight Shoemakers employed in their trade, hath forty Negro Servants, bringing them up in Trades in his house . . . hath abundance of Kine, a brave Dairy, Swine great store, and Poltry."

Colonial and plantation culture reached its peak in such estates as Stratford, owned by the Lees, who ". . . lived here in great state, and kept a band of musicians to whose airs his (Philip Ludwell Lee) daughters, Matilda and Flora, with their companions, danced in the saloon or promenaded on the housetop."

Even smaller landholders fared well, as M. Durand wrote, "The land is so rich and so fertile that when a man has fifty acres of ground, two men-servants, a maid and some cattle, neither he nor his wife do anything but visit among their neighbors. . . ."

23

Of course, the vast number of Virginians of those days were far less fortunate. The wealth of the plantations was built on the unceasing labor of the slaves, who had almost no hope of any better life. Much of the good life of the plantations depended on skilled Negro servants and artisans who could provide the decorations, deliciously prepared food and drink, and other necessities of cultured living. There were also free Negroes who in some ways had a more difficult time than the slaves. Small landholders, merchants and shopkeepers, artisans and tradesmen and the "common" people often had little more joy in life than the slaves.

Eyes on the Frontier

During the first half of the 1700's the frontier had been pushing westward. In 1738 Augusta County was formed. On paper this enormous tract extended from the Blue Ridge to the Mississippi and from the Great Lakes to North Carolina.

Since this land was also claimed by the French, there was growing trouble as the English moved in. The French did everything they could to encourage the Indians to attack English settlers. These difficulties at last grew into what we know as the French and Indian War.

This war brought to prominence a young Virginia officer and aristocrat named George Washington. He did much to save the British from defeat in the wilderness of Pennsylvania and Maryland. For Virginia's defense Washington built Fort Loudoun, near present Winchester, which the French said could never be captured. After demonstrating his ability in many ways, Washington was named commander in chief of the royal forces in Virginia, the first of the long series of high honors that would be his.

The Indian wars brought much terror and suffering to the people of the frontier. In stealthy attacks the Indians burned homesteads, killed settlers, carried off prisoners, killed or captured livestock and in a hundred ways kept the people in constant fear.

One of the strange experiences of the period was that of the Brubakers, who lived near present Luray. One evening Mrs. Brubaker had a vision that Indians would attack. It was so vivid that she could count the number of Indians as they were camped on a nearby mountain. Her vision

24

showed that they would attack the next morning, and she persuaded her husband to take the family to a place where they could be safe. Their neighbors, the Stones, made fun of this prophecy, but the attack took place just as Mrs. Brubaker had foretold; Stone was killed, and his family carried off as captives.

Although the French and Indian War was officially over by 1763, attacks by the Indians continued through much of the Revolutionary War.

Prelude to Freedom

In order to pay the expenses of the French and Indian War, the British government placed "stamp" taxes on several kinds of items used in the colonies. The Virginia General Assembly passed the "Virginia Resolves," which pointed out the injustice in placing taxes on the colonies when they had no voice in whether or not the law would be passed. The most notable leader in calling for the Virginia Resolves was young Patrick Henry, who stirred tremendous excitement when he roared, "Caesar had his Brutus, Charles I his Cromwell, and George III—" At this point many feared the youthful orator might be accused of treason, but he ended safely and cleverly by saying, "may profit from their example." This has been called the "first frank challenge to the King."

The Stamp Taxes were repealed, but after a year others were levied and dissatisfaction grew in Virginia and the other colonies. In 1773, a group of Virginians, including Thomas Jefferson, Richard Henry Lee, Patrick Henry and George Mason, persuaded the Virginia General Assembly to set up a Committee of Correspondence to work with the other colonies to protect their interests.

The hated taxes were repealed except for the tax on tea, but this failed to satisfy the colonists, and Virginia had its own "tea party" as did the other colonies. The First Continental Congress was organized, and Peyton Randolph of Virginia was chosen as its president.

Although haughty Governor Dunmore had dissolved the Virginia General Assembly, Virginians met in several conventions. At the second convention Patrick Henry in a fiery speech called for the arming of the militia as he orated, "Gentlemen may cry 'Peace! Peace!' but there is no peace. The war is actually begun! . . . Is life so dear or peace so sweet as to be purchased at the price of chains and slavery? Forbid it, Almighty God! I know not what course others may take," and then he closed with the familiar words, "but, as for me, give me liberty, or give me death!"

When Governor Dunmore took the public gunpowder from the arsenal, Patrick Henry organized a small army and forced the governor to pay for the powder. Lord Dunmore declared Henry to be an outlaw and the governor later fled to a warship.

On June 15, 1775, Virginia's own George Washington accepted the call of the Continental Congress as commander in chief of all American forces. He hurried to Boston to take command of his untrained troops. The scene had been set for revolution.

Collecting Your Thoughts

Read more detailed accounts of the period and list as many as you can of the steps in Virginia history which led to the break with England.

From Boston to Yorktown

The first armed clash of the Revolutionary War in Virginia took place at Great Bridge on December 9, 1775, when Virginia militia defeated Lord Dunmore.

On May 6, 1776, the Fifth Virginia Convention meeting at Williamsburg declared the colony to be a free and independent commonwealth. On June 7, Richard Henry Lee of Virginia suggested to the Continental Congress that it accept a declaration of independence. On June 12, the Virginia convention adopted George Mason's Bill of Rights and then adopted a constitution which lasted more than 50 years. The Virginia bill of rights was later used as a model for the United States Bill of Rights.

In 1778 Virginia played an unusual part in the war by supporting George Rogers Clark as he made the western frontiers safe against the British. The next year Thomas Jefferson succeeded Patrick Henry as governor. The war came to Virginia in earnest that year when Sir George Collier sailed into Hampton Roads and raided the countryside around Portsmouth. In 1780 there were raids by General Alexander Leslie and Benedict Arnold, who burned part of Richmond.

On May 20, 1781, Lord Charles Cornwallis arrived in Virginia and soon, with 7,000 men, began to pursue General Lafayette, who was defending Virginia. After Lafayette had been joined by General "Mad" Anthony Wayne, they began to push Cornwallis, who finally arrived at Yorktown and fortified it.

Meanwhile, the American forces had been strengthened by 3,000 French troops from Admiral de Grasse, and General Washington decided on an all-out effort in Virginia. Washington and Rochambeau were able to bring the greatest possible numbers of their troops to Virginia in an amazingly short time—one of the great forced marches of history. Admiral de Grasse defeated the British navy and kept it from bringing reinforcements to Cornwallis.

The British in Yorktown were completely surrounded and a long siege began. General Thomas Nelson gladly shelled his own house when it was occupied by the British. One of the most thrilling individual actions in the siege and battle occurred when young Colonel Alexander Hamilton stormed and seized an enemy redoubt.

27

Unable to escape from Yorktown, Cornwallis at last sent his representatives to the Moore house to arrange for his surrender, October 18, 1781. On a broad plain near Yorktown the endless rows of British soldiers marched out, their red coats gleaming, to lay down their arms, while a military band blared the appropriate tune, *The World Turned Upside Down.*

After six years of struggle against seemingly hopeless odds, the skill and will of General Washington and his many comrades in arms had achieved final victory for American independence. It seemed fitting somehow that this should occur at Yorktown in his own Virginia.

Statehood

After another six years in which the inefficient Articles of Confederation provided rules for governing the newly formed country, a group of American leaders met at a convention in Philadelphia. The move to form a new government had been encouraged and fostered by many prominent Virginians, including Washington and James Madison. Jefferson did not take part because he was serving in Europe at the time.

Washington was made president of the convention, and James Madison has been called the "Father" of the American constitution. However, there were many things about the new government which the Virginia delegates did not like. They wanted a bill of rights much like their own; they wanted import of slaves to be stopped immediately as well as other changes.

Although Virginia wanted at least 40 amendments to the new constitution and there was a good deal of opposition to approving it, the new government was finally accepted by Virginia in June, 1788, and the Commonwealth of Virginia became the tenth state of the United States of America. George Washington became the first in an historic succession of the Presidents of that land.

Gains and Setbacks

Little more than a year after Virginia joined the Union, the Commonwealth made a generous contribution to the new nation—a sizeable

WHITE HOUSE
EARLY 1800's

tract of land along the Potomac at Alexandria to be used for a new
national capital. In 1792 another large tract of land was lopped off when
Kentucky, formerly a Virginia county, became a state.

The leadership of Virginia shone in the first years of the new nation
as one Virginian after another led the nation as President—Washington, Jefferson, Madison, Monroe—an unbroken line separated only by
New Englander John Adams.

29

During the War of 1812 a number of Virginia communities and plantations were attacked and pillaged. However, attempted invasions at Norfolk and Portsmouth were driven off. One of the most interesting happenings of the war occurred when President Madison and his wife Dolly fled to Virginia to escape the British capture of Washington. Dolly Madison brought with her the things she had been able to save before the White House was burned, including a copy of the Declaration of Independence and the famed portrait of George Washington.

The period which followed was mainly one of improvement of communications, consolidation and change within the state, a time in which much of the eastern land had been used up and abandoned, and the western areas progressed rapidly. Developments in agriculture, manufacture, education and other fields are discussed in later sections.

The Gathering Clouds

There is a strange irony in the fact that a Virginia Negro, Anthony Johnson, held the first slave in Virginia. The number of slaves increased greatly. In 1860 there were 52,168 Virginians who held slaves, although many leading Virginians were bitterly against the "lifelong ordeal" of slavery. In his first draft of the Declaration of Independence, Thomas Jefferson denounced slavery, saying that the king had "waged cruel war against human nature itself, violating its most sacred right of life and liberty in the person of a distant people who never offended him, captivating and carrying them into slavery in another hemisphere." This wording was cut out of the Declaration by South Carolina and Georgia.

Virginia's George Mason refused to sign the Constitution of the United States because it did not condemn slavery. Elizabeth Russell, sister of Patrick Henry, freed her slaves, saying, ". . . that it is both sinful and unjust, as they are by nature equally free as myself, to continue them in slavery. I do, therefore, by these presents . . . make free the said Negroes."

John Hartwell Cocke of Dixie condemned slavery as "the great cause of all the great evils of our lands."

In 1778 Virginia became the first government in the world to make the slave trade a criminal offense. Emancipation of Virginia's Negroes was almost voted in 1832. The Virginia branch of the American Colonization Society was able to send 243 free Negroes to Liberia in Africa in a single year. Monrovia in Liberia was named in honor of James Monroe.

Most of the abolitionists, who opposed slavery, in Virginia lived in the western section. However, even in the east some risked their safety to help Negroes. Shoe dealer James A. Smith shipped Henry Brown to freedom in the North, completely encased in a box labeled "shoes." Smith was later caught trying to free two other Negroes in the same way and was sent to prison.

However, in spite of some opposition to slavery, the majority of Virginians supported it or felt that any effort in the North to do away with slavery was unjustified interference with the South's affairs. Large profits were made by those who raised and sold slaves like cattle, giving much of eastern Virginia a reputation as a "breeder of slaves."

Virginia—Like a Stone Wall

Virginian Edmund Riffin was given the privilege of firing the first shot at Fort Sumter, which provided the signal for war. When Virginia seceded from the Union on April 17, 1861, "ten thousand hurrahing men and boys carried torches" around Richmond. Fireworks burst above the city, and there was much celebration. Richmond became the capital city of the Confederacy on May 29.

The South won its first great victory on July 21, 1861, in the Battle of Manassas, also known as the first Battle of Bull Run (the stream running through the battlefield). In this battle General Barnard E. Bee marveled at the courage of one of his fellow officers, Thomas Jonathan Jackson, and gave him an immortal nickname when he exclaimed, "There stands Jackson like a stone wall." Stonewall Jackson he has been to history ever since.

Virginia might have been given the same nickname, for she stood like a stone wall in the defense of the Confederacy through four brave and desperate years. Virginia was the key battleground of the war. The Winchester area alone was the scene of over 100 engagements. The city of Fredericksburg changed hands seven times. The Shenandoah Valley became the "pathway of war."

Union troops occupied Alexandria and western Virginia (which became the state of West Virginia on June 20, 1863). The South prepared for a great attack from the north. One of the most interesting of these preparations was the converting of the ship *Merrimac* into an iron-covered warship known as the *Virginia*. On March 8, 1862, the *Virginia* sank several Union war ships. On the next day the *Virginia* met another new type of boat, nicknamed a cheesebox on a raft because of its shape—the *Monitor*.

Through a four-hour period the two ships pounded each other in a battle that is said to have completely altered naval warfare. "Tactically, it was a drawn fight," said R. S. Henry, "in its results a victory for the *Monitor*."

Important military movements began on land in Virginia at about the same time. Union General George McClellan began a march on Richmond, and in May he came within sight of the Confederate capital. Then one of the great military leaders of all time—Robert Edward Lee—was placed in comand of the Confederate army in Virginia. Norfolk fell to Union forces on May 10, and the Union fleet tried to help the attack on Richmond but was stopped at Drewry's Bluff. Then Lee drove McClellan back from Richmond and saved the Confederate capital.

After this he turned to meet an attack in the Shenandoah Valley. There General Stonewall Jackson carried on a campaign that has been called "a model of military strategy," holding the valley against heavy odds. One of Jackson's most amazing accomplishments was moving 22,000 men in a tremendous march of 56 miles in two days to encircle the Union army.

The forces of General John Pope lost the second Battle of Manassas, July 29-30, 1862, and in the Battle of Fredericksburg, December 13, 1862, Union forces had 12,653 killed and Confederates, 5,377.

Union forces marched south again in 1863. At Chancellorsville on

May 2 and 3 General Lee defeated the forces of General Joseph Hooker, forces numbering more than twice his own. However, this was the last of the long series of Union disasters. The South lost its "stone wall" during this battle when General Jackson was shot by his own forces who did not recognize him in the dusk. Many have said that this was a loss from which the South could never quite recover.

After General Ulysses S. Grant was made Union commander, he and General George G. Meade turned toward Virginia. On May 4 the Wilderness Battle began an 11-month campaign to decide the fate of Virginia. Beginning May 8 the five-day Battle of Spotsylvania Courthouse brought some of the bloodiest fighting of the entire war.

In order to defend Richmond, Confederate forces had arranged three separate rings of defense. The inner defense included 25 separate forts and strong points. There was an intermediate line of breastworks and finally an outer line. One of the keys to this defense was the railroad center of Petersburg. Unable to capture Petersburg, Grant began what became a long and terrible siege of the city.

All attempts to break through the defenses of Richmond failed the Union forces in 1864. Then in the spring of 1865 Grant began his final drive. On April 2 came the first break in Lee's line—southwest of Richmond; although the second line of Richmond's defenses was never conquered, on April 3 Confederate forces and civilians were removed from Petersburg and Richmond.

The next day Richmond was burned by its own people to keep everything useful out of Union hands. These "self-set flames mounted like a funeral pyre to the cause for which it had sacrificed so much."

For the period of April 3 to 10, Danville was the capital of the dying Confederacy. Here President Jefferson Davis held the last full meetings of his cabinet.

Grant continued to pursue Lee's forces until April 9. The exhausted, starving, poorly equipped remnants of the once mighty Confederate army, camped near Appomattox Courthouse, saw no other course except surrender.

General Lee found a sparkling new uniform and went to the living room of the Wilmer McLean house near the courthouse. Shortly afterward General Grant hurried up; he apologized for his appearance to his old acquaintance, General Lee. To save Lee's time Grant had rushed in from the field, dusty and unkempt, with no chance to change his uniform. Grant may have remembered the occasion during the Mexican War when Lee had reprimanded him for his untidy appearance. The southern general inquired what surrender terms Grant might offer, and the northern commander sat down at the small table to write: A deep silence followed, during which only the scratching of the pen could be heard.

General Lee felt that the terms were most generous. The men would not be held as prisoners but would be paroled if they promised not to go to war again against the Union. Only the property of the Confederate government or other public property would have to be surrendered. Since the horses were almost all the property of the men, they would have them for the spring plowing. Grant further ordered his men to supply rations for 25,000 men so that the Confederate soldiers need not starve.

When news of the surrender came, Grant's troops were ready for a tremendous victory celebration, but General Grant refused to let them do anything that would make the Confederate forces more bitter. He hoped that in the McLean house and the surrounding area that day the first steps had been taken to reunite in a humane way the separated and brutally suffering nation.

Awful Aftermath

This hope was not to be; with the assassination of President Abraham Lincoln, those who felt the South must pay bitterly for the war gained their way. Attempts were made at various times to regain the power of a civilian government for Virginia. However, for most of the time between the end of the war and 1870, Virginia was under repressive Federal military control.

In July, 1869, the people voted to approve a new constitution. They rejected clauses which took the vote away from Confederate military officers and which prohibited anyone from holding office who had helped the Confederacy. The new legislature met under this constitution and approved the 14th and 15th amendments to the United States Constitution. On January 26, 1870, Virginia once again became a sovereign state. Virginians had some sense of satisfaction in the fact that the radicals had never controlled the Old Dominion.

However wartime troubles were not over. Most of the wealth of Virginia had been poured into the war effort. Plantations and farms had been left in ruin, without even seeds to plant or livestock to raise. Railways were wrecked or in bad repair. Manufacturing plants had been demolished by Union troops to keep them from turning out war supplies, or by the Confederates to keep them from falling into Union hands. Private and public debts appeared to be so huge that they could never be repaid. West Virginia, which had become a separate state, refused to pay its share of debts dating before the war. In spite of Federal efforts to help Negroes, great numbers of them were in terrible need; they had been cut off from their old life with almost no opportunities to work toward a new life.

Turmoil was continued as General William Mahone gained great political power and became in a sense a political boss of the state until 1883. The period was one of corruption and injustice.

A Modern State

In spite of all of these difficulties, progress was made in education, manufacturing, agriculture, transportation and communication, and something like the old prosperity began to appear in scattered areas.

In 1894 the boundary line between Maryland and Virginia on the Delmarva Peninsula was settled; this had been disputed for more than 200 years, since the first settlement. Another boundary, that with North Carolina and Tennessee, had been in question for more than a hundred years when it was settled in 1903 by the United States Supreme Court.

In 1901 a convention met to write a new constitution. This was never approved by the voters, but in 1902 was "proclaimed" at the convention and "approved" by the legislature. Although it improved the old constitution in many ways, it provided means by which poor and illiterate voters, both white and Negro but especially Negro, were kept from voting. Voters had to pass an intelligence test and pay a three-year poll tax in advance.

35

In Staunton came another government change that had far-reaching effects. The city manager plan was first used in that city in 1908, and the pattern set in a Virginia community has been copied by many cities all over the world.

Virginia-born Thomas Woodrow Wilson was inaugurated as President in 1913 for an administration dominated by World War I. In that war, prosperity came to Virginia, with wartime industries and great military establishments in the commonwealth. The Newport News Shipbuilding and Dry Dock Company built 20 per cent of all the tonnage of the United States Navy in World War I. During the war fifty thousand troops were trained at Camp Lee, one of the largest in the country. Camp Stuart, where troops were shipped out; Camp Humphrey, training engineers; and Langley Field, one of the country's main aviation centers, were other busy military centers.

In the war 91,623 from Virginia were in the armed services, and 1,635 lost their lives.

When Henry Flood Byrd was governor, the state government was entirely reorganized in 1927 to simplify and improve government service

to the people. However, the constitution was not completely rewritten at this time.

One of the nation's most popular national parks was established in Virginia in 1935 under the name of Shenandoah National Park.

During World War II, 214,903 Virginian men and women saw service. The Newport News shipyard built 185 ships for wartime uses.

After the war much of the state forged ahead in an amazing rise in population, prosperity, growth of the city and other ways. Lagging behind was the mountain section. In March of 1965 the Appalachian Regional Development Act of the Federal government came into being to encourage the development of this area. Another far-reaching development occurred in education in 1966 when the State Department of Community Colleges was established to develop two-year branches of major colleges in the state, to bring higher education within commuting distance of almost every high school graduate of the commonwealth.

The People of the Old Dominion

The founders of Virginia were English, but it was not long before those of other backgrounds began to come to the Old Dominion. After 1685 French refugees became the largest early group of these. Large numbers of German and Scottish people settled in the mountain regions, and many of their descendants are among the mountain people today. While there are in Virginia today people with backgrounds of almost every country, the commonwealth has never been the "melting pot" of some other states.

The Church of England (Episcopal) was the established church of Virginia. On many occasions those who professed other faiths were persecuted or driven away. However, eventually those of other beliefs were tolerated—Catholics, Presbyterians, Quakers, Baptists and others. Virginia's first Jewish congregation was established in 1789.

Volumes could be written, and many have been, about the proud and courageous mountain people of Virginia, about their hard life and colorful customs and mannerisms. As television, fast roads, better education and other "space-age advantages" reach into even the most remote areas, these "differences" are gradually dying out, although much of the

generous hospitality remains in the highland regions.

In spite of the fact that much of the wealth and success of Virginia as a state has been due to the toil of Negro workers, recognition and success have been slow in coming to them. Many individuals did achieve fame and success, however, and some of these are discussed in a later chapter. There were 816,258 Negro residents of Virginia listed in the 1960 census.

Only a handful, 2,155, Indians remained in Virginia, according to the 1960 census, to remind today's people of proud Powhatan who once ruled the region in primitive splendor and of the other Indian peoples.

As Virginia moves into the last part of the twentieth century it seems likely that all races and groups, in spite of dissension and difficulties, have laid a foundation on which solid progress can be built.

Collecting Your Thoughts

If a television producer planned to broadcast a program on the most interesting event in Virginia history, what event do you think he would select?

In spite of more than 300 years of use, the forests of Virginia still cover 63 per cent of the commonwealth. Land which is not of use for anything else is being restored to forests at the rate of 100,000 acres a year. Although the vast reaches of pine forests are growing smaller, the acreage of hardwoods is increasing with a "striking" growth. Two national forests, George Washington and Jefferson, help to conserve and promote the best uses of the forest resources.

The amount of smaller plant life in the state is shown by the fact that the Galax-Hillsville area is said to have the largest variety of plant life in the United States. Among Virginia's more unusual plants are the lotus and the galax. The lotus gardens of Virginia Beach are the last large stands of the American lotus in the country. The galax is a distinctive and handsome mountain evergreen.

Many kinds of wild life have disappeared—buffalo, wolves, panthers and others—but a variety of animals and birds still survives, including the wild ponies of Chincoteague Island. These are not true ponies but a kind of stunted horse.

Mineral riches of Virginia include coal, sandstone, limestone, black marble, shale, dolomite, greenstone, soapstone, feldspar, mica, marl, granite, brick clays, gypsum, barite, glass sand, salt, cyanide, iron, manganese, zinc, lead, graphite, titanium, phyrrhotite, pyrite and even gold. The strain of gold-bearing rock runs through the central Piedmont area. More unusual minerals include aplite, ilmenite, rutile, and kyanite.

One of the unique agencies which helps Virginia preserve its natural treasures is the Virginia Natural Areas System.

Collecting Your Thoughts

Choose one of the natural resources of Virginia and find how it is being protected and wisely used.

People Use Their Treasures

Mother of Manufacturing

Manufacturing in the world's greatest manufacturing country was begun in Virginia in 1608 by the Jamestown colonists. They built a glass factory. Visitors to Jamestown today can see the first primitive factory reproduced. Here knicker-clad workers puff out their cheeks to blow the glass just as they did in the early days.

America's first iron furnace was set up in 1619 by John Berkeley near present Chesterfield. Richard Dawson of Gloucester County was the first man in America to "make money" when he struck the country's first coins.

There were many water-powered grain and saw mills. George Washington proudly claimed that the flour made in his mill was "equal in quality to any made in this country."

Today the value of Virginia manufacturing is more than three billion dollars a year. Chemical and textile industries are the largest employers in the commonwealth. Virginia ranks first among all the states in the production of synthetic fibers, turning out a mammoth 25 per cent of all such materials produced in the country.

Wood products alone in Virginia are worth $700,000,000 a year. Furniture mogul John David Bassett created the world's largest wood furniture producing empire, with headquarters at Bassett, Virginia. This one company turns out more than 55 per cent of all the wood furniture made in the United States. Wood milling remains one of the state's important industries, with 1,600 saw and planing mills operating in the commonwealth.

The largest single manufacturing firm in the state is the gigantic Newport News Shipbuilding and Dry Dock Company. This has long been one of the most unusual firms. Its founder, famed industrialist Collis Potter Huntington, poured more than $10,000,000 into the shipyard without ever realizing a cent of income from its operation before his death in 1900. He was content to say: "We build good ships here at a profit if we can, at a loss if we must, but always good ships."

Those "good ships" have included the mammoth aircraft super-carrier *Enterprise,* first nuclear powered carrier and largest ship in the world, and the Atlantic record-holder passenger liner *United States.* Thirteen

nuclear powered submarines have also slid into the waters from the Newport News ways. The plant is considered to be the largest privately owned shipyard in the world.

Babcock and Wilcox of Lynchburg is the world's leading producer of steam generating equipment. They have now also become experts in the highly specialized skill of producing commercial type atomic power plants. One of their accomplishments in this field was the power plant for our first nuclear cargo ship, *Savannah*.

Another Virginia company ranks as one of the three largest processors of frozen foods in the United States. This is the Morton company of Crozet. A small but interesting part of the food field is the Smithfield ham business. More than 350 years ago the Indians taught the colonists how to cure the hams from razorback hogs, using hickory smoke. Today Smithfield is known as the "hickory smoking capital of the world," and some say there is nothing to equal the taste of a Virginia ham.

Virginia's 10,000 fishermen have a catch valued at $24,200,000 a year. The James River is especially famous for its oystering—producing a plump bivalve that is one of the most delicious found anywhere.

Seeking and Finding—Research

Virginia is a leader among the southern states in scientific research. One of the most recent major developments in this field is the $14,200,000 Space Radiation Effects Laboratory which went into operation near Newport News in 1966 as a project of National Aeronautics and Space Administration. Space Radiation Effects Laboratory is a part of a unique scientific agency known as Virginia Associated Research Center, operated jointly by the College of William and Mary, the University of Virginia and Virginia Polytechnic Institute.

"One of the five major science centers of the United States," according to the Virginia Industrial Development and Planning Division, is the Atlantic Research Corporation, founded in 1949 by Dr. Arthur Sloan and Dr. Arch Scurlock. It is located about five miles south of Washington. One of their principal projects is the development of solid fuels for rockets.

This searching for new facts and ideas is in the Virginia tradition. One of the most far-reaching inventions in the world's history was developed in the Old Dominion. Working on his farm, Walnut Grove, near Greenville, Cyrus Hall McCormick perfected in 1831 a machine which would cut and gather grain mechanically. At that time he was only 22. By 1847 he had sold only 778 of his reapers and moved west to be nearer the grain country.

At Raphine Hall, near Walnut Grove, James Ethan Allen Gibbs is credited with inventing in 1857 a particular kind of the sewing machine —the "twisted loop rotary hook" type.

42

Agriculture

Total agricultural income of Virginia was estimated at $567,800,000 in 1965. Livestock and crops are almost equally balanced in providing farm income—$249,900,000 for livestock and $249,700,000 for crops.

Tobacco brings in almost a third of the Virginia farmer's crop money. When John Rolfe began the country's first experiment in tobacco raising, he was quite satisfied with his efforts and described his tobacco as "strong, sweet and pleasant as any under the sun." Danville is one of the famous centers of tobacco growing in the South, noted for its bright leaf, and the Danville and South Boston tobacco auctions rank among the most important.

There is great variety in Virginia's agriculture. The truck farms of the Eastern Shore produce fresh vegetables and small fruits on a large scale; inland from Norfolk, peanuts, soybeans, and hogs are the major items. Virginia peanut crops in 1964 totalled 210,080,000 pounds as compared with 172,083,000 for tobacco. However, income from peanuts ($30,607,-000) is little more than a third of that from tobacco ($85,022,000).

The Valley of Virginia is one of the nation's most important apple-growing regions. In Frederick County alone more than 700,000 apple trees in the spring blanket the countryside with pink and white bloom. The Albemarle pippin apple was said to have been a favorite of Queen Victoria, who often sent for supplies of them to be delivered to the palace.

In many counties of Virginia there has been a change-over from field crops to dairy and beef cattle. Dairy products in Virginia amount to $94,402,000, cattle and calves $70,660,000. Broiler chickens alone brought $23,157,000 to Virginia farmers in 1965.

A "crop" which most people would not expect to find in Virginia is maple syrup, with a small industry centered in Highland County.

Cotton is no longer a principal Virginia crop. At one time many people held great hope for the silk industry, and mulberry trees and silk worms were brought in very early. Virginia silkworms spun 300 pounds of silk which Governor William Berkeley proudly sent to King Charles II for the royal coronation robes, but the silk industry did not succeed in Virginia.

43

Today's agriculture owes much to the foundation laid by generations· of Virginia farmers large and small.

Mining and Minerals

Mineral production in Virginia in 1965 was valued at $242,000,000.

The first commercial coal mining operation in the United States began in Virginia in 1750. Today coal is the leading mineral industry of the state; the commonwealth is sixth in coal among all the states. One coal mining operation near Lebanon is considered the largest in the world.

Stone quarried in Virginia in 1965 brought $51,915,000. Sand and gravel produced in the state ranks third in value of the state's minerals. Zinc is the leading metallic mineral produced in the commonwealth. Lead has long been important, even before the Fort Chiswell lead mines supplied bullets for the Revolution.

Transportation and Communication

One of the world's most spectacular highways for the first time in history linked Virginia's eastern peninsula with the rest of the Old Dominion by road. This was the Chesapeake Bay Bridge-Tunnel. To build this 23-mile-long marvel, engineers constructed four artificial "islands" in the middle of the bay. These islands anchored the ends of the bridges and provided entrances for two tunnels which burrow beneath the bay. These tunnels left two wide channels in the bay for the passage of ships. With this construction no possible disaster could close vital Hampton Roads to naval ships.

Spectacular as it is, this is only one part of the state roads and highways in Virginia totalling 50,000 miles. The commonwealth ranks third among

BAY BRIDGE

all the states in total mileage of state administered roads and streets. When the great interstate road system is completed, Virginia will have 1,056 miles of these superhighways, connecting almost every community of more than 5,000 population in the state.

Virginia's first railroad (the Chesterfield Railroad) began operating in 1831. Its cars were drawn by horses, carrying coal over the 13 miles from the mines to Richmond. Each car held only 56 bushels of coal. In 1836 the first passenger railroad, the Richmond, Fredericksburg and Potomac Railroad, carried frightened passengers across the country at the breath-taking speed of ten miles per hour.

Today Virginia has 4,078 miles of railroad tracks. Included in these are part of the lines of the Norfolk and Western, with headquarters in Virginia. Financial experts consider the Norfolk and Western to be at present the most profitable of all the major railroads in the country.

The Norfolk-Hampton Roads area has been under the influence of commerce from the sea ever since the first merchants dropped anchor there nearly 300 years ago. The Hampton Roads shipping center includes Newport News, Portsmouth and Chesapeake in addition to Norfolk. Among other distinctions, Hampton Roads leads all other United States ports in coal dumping and is the leading Atlantic coast port in the export of grain. Over 5,000 ships a year call at Hampton Roads. A new $15,000,000 general cargo pier has been completed recently. Norfolk has become a major crossroads of international commerce in modern times.

Virginia's international shipping operations are supervised by the Virginia State Ports Authority. Virginia exports in 1964 totaled $1,012,725,616.

The country's first canal was opened in 1790, connecting Richmond with Westham, running parallel with the James River for seven miles. The James Company which built this canal was sponsored by George Washington, John Marshall, Edmund Randolph and other prominent men. The old Potomac Canal, also sponsored by Washington, was a forerunner of the later Chesapeake and Ohio Canal. In 1812 a canal cutting through the Dismal Swamp linked the waters of Chesapeake Bay and Albemarle Sound.

Commercial steamboats began operation to Virginia ports in 1813.

DULLES INTERNATIONAL AIRPORT

Vast Dulles International Airport at Chantilly, with its pagoda-shaped control tower and swooping main building, heads the list of Virginia's 76 airports. Dulles is one of the world's largest flying fields.

Virginia possesses one of the true distinctions in the newspaper field. The Alexandria *Gazette* is the nation's oldest continuously operating daily paper. It is the continuation of the Virginia *Journal* and Alexandria *Advertiser,* started in 1784. The Virginia *Gazette* of Williamsburg, a weekly, was the first newspaper to be published in the commonwealth.

Collecting Your Thoughts

If you had your choice of entering a business or taking up an occupation in Virginia today which would you think would offer you the most opportunity? Be most interesting?

Proud Presidential Parent

Eight American Presidents were born in Virginia. Ohio, which also is known as the "mother of Presidents," claims eight Presidents, too, but one is William Henry Harrison, who was born in Virginia. However, it must be added that some of the Virginia-born Presidents spent much of their lives and gained their fame outside the state.

The early Presidents were probably most truly sons of the Old Dominion. In fact, the first four—Washington, Jefferson, Madison and Monroe—are known as "the Virginia Dynasty."

His Country's Father

Although George Washington has been given much fame as the Father of His Country, few people today properly recognize the greatness of this really magnificent man. Fewer still realize that he was a lively and vital person of keen wit and unusual humor and wide capacity for understanding.

After Jane Butler Washington, first wife of Augustine Washington, died, Augustine married Mary Ball of Sandy Point. Their first child was born February 22, 1732, and named George. When George was 16 he went to live with his half-brother Lawrence, who had built a house called Mount Vernon on the Hunting Creek plantation, first owned by the family's founder in America, in 1669.

Lawrence planned to enlist George in the British Navy, but Mary Ball Washington heard of this and promptly brought her son back to the Ferry Farm near Fredericksburg where her husband had settled his family several years before his death. The history of the world might have been changed if George Washington had become a British naval officer.

In 1748 the powerful Lord Fairfax hired youthful George Washington to survey his enormous estate, and Washington set out, admiring the scenery as he passed "through most beautiful groves of Sugar Trees and spent ye best part of ye Day in admiring ye Trees and richness of ye Land."

Such things always interested Washington; his great ambition was to

GARDEN
MOUNT VERNON

become the foremost agriculturist in America, and his many experiments and advanced farming (including the then little-known rotation of crops) and livestock methods in later life may have qualified him for that title. On the lighter side, he even once won a prize for "raising the largest jackass." However, much higher prizes were in store for him.

Demonstrating his exceptional military and organizational abilities in the Indian wars, Washington next received political know-how as a member of the House of Burgesses. The House passed resolutions to thank Washington for his service in the Indian wars, but when he rose to speak he was too embarrassed to find the words. John Robinson, the Speaker of the House, said, "Sit down, Mr. Washington. Your modesty surpasses your valor, and that is beyond any language at my command."

In the Revolution it is probable that no other man in America could have kept together the disorganized, poorly trained, often starving, military forces of the newborn country. Time and again only the calm persuasion of the commander in chief and his eloquent pleas for money and food and other support kept the Revolution going.

When Washington was President of the Constitutional Convention, that same calm manner soothed many controversies and paved the way for a strong government, a legacy we still have of the convention's work. Would the new government have been able to endure the turmoil and disagreements, the bitter battles among those who disagreed with it, if it had not been for that same calm judgment and vast experience during Washington's two terms as President? Many authorities believe it would not.

The complications of putting into operation a form of government completely new in world history in a poverty stricken, war-ravaged, disorganized country composed of separate states jealous of their rights was almost beyond imagination. Yet when Washington had served two terms and refused a third, he was able to pass on to John Adams a government that was running quite smoothly and with great promise of things to come. Washington was the only President ever to receive the unanimous vote of the Electoral College.

Washington returned to Mount Vernon in 1797, which he had inherited from Lawrence, his half-brother, to work on his beloved agriculture, possibly with hopes that he might be able to fulfill his long-time ambition to learn to play the flute and to enjoy other pleasures that his life of service for his country had never permitted.

In 1752 Washington had proposed to Miss Elizabeth Fauntleroy, but she had coolly turned him down because of the smallpox marks on his face. He had written a touching letter to her father, saying, "I propose . . . to wait on Miss Betsy, in hopes of a revocation of the former cruel sentence and see if I can meet with any alteration in my favor." But this was not to be.

When he married Martha Custis his bride had two children. Martha Parke Custis died in her teens without marrying. John Parke Custis lived until just after the Revolutionary War and left a widow and four children. Both the Washingtons were terribly grieved, and at John's

49

deathbed Washington said to John's wife Eleanor, "I adopt the two youngest children as my own."

These children were Eleanor Parke Custis and George Washington Parke Custis, who were raised at Mount Vernon. Some histories refer to them as foster children or adopted grandchildren of the Washingtons; however, they probably should be called simply adopted children. Both were very much cherished, especially Washington's beloved Nelly Custis.

Washington was to have only two quiet years at home after his Presidency. He made one of his regular trips to his mill, caught a cold and died on December 14, 1799.

"Mr. Jefferson"

If Thomas Jefferson had not won even greater fame in other fields, he would certainly still have great renown as one of this country's leading architects; even without his other accomplishments he would be recognized as a leading writer; his achievements in education place him in the rank of leading educators. Given more time he probably would have become an outstanding inventor. Like Benjamin Franklin, Jefferson was one of the most versatile of all widely-known Americans.

Thomas Jefferson was born April 13, 1743, at Shadwell, the farm of his father, Peter Jefferson, not far from where the son later built his Monticello estate. He was educated at William and Mary College, gained his political experience first in the House of Burgesses.

Possibly his greatest fame came at the age of 33 when he drafted the ringing phrases of the Declaration of Independence, and established his reputation as one of the great social and political philosophers of all time. As governor of Virginia following Patrick Henry, he was not especially distinguished. He became minister to France, following Benjamin Franklin, and saw the horrors of the beginning of the French Revolution.

Jefferson served as Washington's Secretary of State, then as Vice President and then as President, winning the post from Aaron Burr through only one vote—that of Alexander Hamilton. As President the highlights of his term were the successful war with the Barbary pirates,

JEFFERSON'S HOME
MONTICELLO

the magnificent purchase of vast Louisiana Territory and the exploration of that territory by his friend Meriwether Lewis with William Clark, both also Virginia natives.

After his second term, Jefferson retired, becoming the "Sage of Monticello." He had barely begun Monticello, near Charlottesville, when he brought his bride there on horseback through a January blizzard in 1772. He did not finish the handsome, ingeniously planned house until 1809. He loved "gadgets" and built dozens of labor-saving devices and curiosities into his home, such as disappearing beds of his own design, dumb-waiters, unique ventilating and lighting systems, unusual clocks and many other things. Among his other accomplishments he improved the design of plow moldboards and demonstrated at Lynchburg that the tomato was not poisonous, as most people had thought.

His fame was so great that many people, sometimes as many as 40 or 50 in a day, visited him at Monticello. He is still known in Charlottesville simply as "Mr. Jefferson." He was so hospitable and generous to the many visitors that he very much reduced his circumstances by the time he died in 1826. His widow was left with comparatively little property. By some strange turn of fortune, the writer of the Declaration of Independence died on the Fourth of July exactly 50 years after it had been first proclaimed.

The epitaph which he wrote for himself simply reads: "Here was buried Thomas Jefferson, author of the Declaration of American Independence, of the statute of Virginia for religious freedom and father of the University of Virginia."

He made no mention of the Presidency or his accomplishments in many fields such as architecture. The Marquis de Chastellux as early as 1782 wrote: "We may safely aver that Mr. Jefferson is the first American who has consulted the fine arts to know how he should shelter himself from the weather." In addition to Monticello his greatest architectural monuments are the early buildings of the University of Virginia and the state capitol. Many of the fine old houses of Virginia were either designed by Jefferson or built following his suggestions.

DOLLY MADISON

Hail to the Chiefs!

The greatest work of James Madison, born at Port Conway, March 16, 1751, lives on today in the finest design of national government ever created—the Constitution of the United States. Because of his work in drafting the Constitution he has become known as the "Father of the Constitution." After the Constitution was operating, Madison introduced the Bill of Rights so that the freedoms implied under the Constitution would be more surely guaranteed.

He served as Secretary of State under Jefferson and was chosen President in 1808. He lost popularity because of his poor handling of the War of 1812, nicknamed "Mr. Madison's War." After his second term, he retired to his estate, Montpelier.

In 1794 Madison married the beautiful widow Dolly Payne. In Washington at the White House and at Montpelier she gained the reputation as one of the most popular and talented hostesses in the history of the country. The Madisons entertained at Montpelier in an especially elaborate manner. James Madison died June 28, 1836.

James Monroe has never received the public recognition he deserves. He fought in the Revolution, served as United States Senator and as minister to France, then as governor of Virginia. He returned to France where he carried out Jefferson's instructions and brilliantly negotiated to buy the Louisiana Territory from Napoleon. He served as Madison's Secretary of State then as Secretary of War.

Monroe was elected President in 1816; during his terms he solved the problem of the border with Canada and made it possible for the long Canadian border to be undefended—one of the true moves for peace of all time. He also managed to settle the border dispute between the United States and Russia in the northwest. Also during his term Florida finally became a part of the United States, completing a project Monroe had not been able to finish when he bought Louisiana.

The best known of his accomplishments came about when he decided, in consultation with his friend and mentor Thomas Jefferson, to try to stop the interference of European governments in the affairs of countries in the Western Hemisphere. President Monroe proclaimed a policy that the United States would protect its neighbors. This policy has come to be known as the Monroe Doctrine. Its effects have been among the most far-reaching in the whole history of diplomatic relations.

Monroe was born in Westmoreland County on April 28, 1758, and died in New York City, strangely, also on the Fourth of July, 1831.

William Henry Harrison was born in Berkeley, Charles City County, February 9, 1773, a son of Benjamin Harrison who was a signer of the Declaration of Independence, one of the long dynasty of Harrisons. He gained most of his fame as governor of the Northwest Territory and as a general in the Indian wars. His victory at the Battle of Tippecanoe in Indiana provided his campaign slogan, "Tippecanoe and Tyler, Too." After his inauguration to the Presidency, he served 31 days and died in office; he never recovered from a cold he caught during his inaugural ceremonies.

Harrison's Vice President was also a Virginian. John Tyler was born March 29, 1790, in Greenway, also in Charles City County, by odd coincidence only a stone's throw away from Harrison's birthplace. He was graduated from William and Mary College, served in the Virginia legislature, then as governor, finally as United States Senator. In 1840 he was elected Vice President and took over the Presidency on the death of Harrison. This first death of a President in office was an historic moment, because there was some question until this time as to whether the Vice President had the right to succeed or a new President would be elected.

By taking over the office, Tyler decided the question. One of the high points of his term as President was the addition of the Republic of Texas as a state. He failed to win nomination for a second term.

Later, Tyler was opposed to secession and tried to keep peace at Fort Sumter. However, when war came he supported the South and died January 18, 1862, before he could take his place in the Confederate Congress.

On November 24, 1784, Zachary Taylor was born in Orange County, but his parents moved to Kentucky when he was only nine months old. Forty years of military service came to its high point in his victories in the war with Mexico, where he became known as "Old Rough and Ready." His wartime popularity carried him into office as the 12th President of the United States, but he had served only 16 months when he died of typhus fever July 9, 1850. Another hero of the Mexican War, Winfield Scott, was also a native of Virginia, born near Petersburg.

The man who became the 28th President, Thomas Woodrow Wilson, was born in the manse of the First Presbyterian Church of Staunton on

WILSON MANSE

December 28, 1856, while his father was the minister there. Except for the period in which he studied law at the University of Virginia, little of Wilson's adult life was spent in his native state. After making a fine reputation as governor of New Jersey, he won his first election to the Presidency over a divided Republican Party. A campaign based on the slogan "He kept us out of war" brought Wilson his second term, and shortly afterward the United States entered World War I.

In order, as he said, to save the world from future wars, Wilson proposed that a League of Nations be formed, but he could not persuade Congress to permit the United States to join the League. Worn out and bitterly disappointed over this struggle, he suffered a stroke and never recovered. His second wife, Edith Bolling Wilson, kept the President away from most of his advisers and government officials during his long illness, and many complained that she had taken on the job of "unofficial President."

When Warren Harding was inaugurated as President, Wilson did make a public appearance. He died February 3, 1924. One of his highest distinctions was the award of the Nobel Prize for Peace in 1919.

Other Public Figures

Patrick Henry, born in Hanover County May 29, 1736, gained early fame as an orator while he practiced law. His voice was so strong it was said he could give orders to his slaves half a mile away. His remarkable personal life included two wives who presented him with 15 children. During his stormy political career his noted speeches gave the English language some of its best known quotations, already referred to.

He served five years as governor of Virginia. One of his greatest accomplishments as governor was authorizing the expedition of George Rogers Clark in Illinois and Indiana (then considered part of Virginia), which won the west for America.

He opposed the Constitution of the United States, but when George Washington appealed to him, one of his last acts was to make a speech at the Charlotte Courthouse for the support of the President and the Federal government. This speech was in the best "fiery" oratory of his earlier days. He died June 6, 1799, just a few months before Washington.

The Lee family was one of the most distinguished in Virginia history. Thomas Lee was the only native Virginian named by the king as a royal governor of Virginia. Richard Henry Lee, a leading figure in the Revolution, and Francis Lightfoot Lee were the only two brothers to sign the Declaration of Independence. "Lighthorse Harry" Lee, spectacular Revolutionary War officer, and governor of Virginia, was the father of the most famous of all the Lees—Robert Edward Lee.

Robert E. Lee was born at Stratford, the elegant plantation of the Lee family. After graduation from West Point, he had many military assignments, including command of the troops that captured John Brown at Harpers Ferry. Abraham Lincoln offered him command of Union troops, but he felt he could not accept and make war on his own people, although he strongly opposed slavery. He once said, " . . . slavery as an institution is a moral and political evil in any country . . . a greater evil to the white than to the black race."

His spectacular triumphs early in the war helped to maintain a strong South, but not even his military genius could overcome the gradual weakening of the Southern forces. When the war was over, he accepted the presidency of Washington College, which later was

ROBERT E. LEE HOME
ARLINGTON HOUSE

renamed Washington and Lee in his honor.

Today this cultured, gentle man of dignity and respect for his fellow man is honored in both North and South for his fine qualities.

Other remarkable Virginia natives with public careers include: Peyton Randolph, first president of the First Continental Congress; William Fleming, only man from west of the Blue Ridge to sit in the Continental Congress; Richard Bland, "great Virginia patriot and statesman;" Sam Houston, only man ever to be governor of two states, president of a republic and United States Senator; Walter Reed, discoverer of the cause of yellow fever; one of America's great military strategists, Thomas Jonathan (Stonewall) Jackson; George Mason, the aristocrat who wrote the bill of rights in the Virginia constitution, a model for that of the United States; Robert "King" Carter, whose descendants number eight governors of Virginia, three signers of the Declaration of Independence, two Presidents, a chief justice, a bishop, and General Robert E. Lee; John Marshall, often listed as our greatest chief justice; and George C. Marshall, one of the best-known men of modern times, architect of America's World War II policies and originator of the Marshall Plan to aid war-torn Europe.

The Princess and the Captain

Two of the most interesting characters of American history are Captain John Smith and the Indian princess Pocahontas. The survival of the first English colony in America was due mostly to the courage, daring and experience of Smith. However, he treated the Indians so harshly that he was probably also responsible for many of the later Indian troubles. In his daring explorations he ranged over much of the coast. He wrote most extraordinary accounts of his explorations: *General Historie of Virginia, A True Relation,* and later after his trip to New England *A Description of New England.*

Pocahontas, supposed to have saved Smith's life, was very much in love with the captain, but he failed to acknowledge this. When she was brought to Jamestown as a captive several years after he went back to England, she was told that Smith was dead. Before marrying John Rolfe, she was baptized and renamed Rebecca. Rolfe took his Indian wife with him to London in 1617, and there she met Smith. He reported, "After a modest salutation, without any word, she turned about, obscured her face, as not seeming well contented; and in that humour . . . we all left her two or three houres, repenting my selfe to have writ she could speake English. But not long after, she began to talke, and remembered mee well what courtesies shee had done. . . ."

Later she sadly said to Smith, " . . . They did tell us alwaies you were dead . . . your Countriemen will lie much."

Although Pocahontas died in London, her son Thomas returned to America, after he grew to manhood in London. He came back to the estate given to his father as a dowry by Emperor Powhatan—the same estate where Rolfe introduced tobacco growing. Thomas Rolfe married Jane Poythress, and they had a large number of descendants. It is interesting to note that the second wife of Woodrow Wilson, Edith Bolling Galt Wilson, was a descendant of Pocahontas through this family.

Creative Virginians

Many famous characters in literature have been "born" in Virginia. The velvet-suited, white-collared hero *Little Lord Fauntleroy* was created by Frances Hodgson Burnett, who said he based him on the son of a friend in Norfolk. The well-loved song character, Sweet Alice, was created by English writer Thomas Dunn while he was a guest in the Peery house near Tazewell. The song, of course, became *Do You Remember Sweet Alice, Ben Bolt?*

Another poet from abroad, Irish Tom Moore, visited Richmond in 1803. His works *The Lake of the Dismal Swamp* and *To the Firefly* were written on this visit. He was much intrigued by fireflies when he saw them for the first time at Williamsburg.

The orphaned Edgar Allan Poe was adopted by the Allans of Richmond. He was educated in Richmond and at the University of Virginia. He later said, "I am a Virginian, at least I call myself one." Other Virginia poets were Father Abraham Joseph Ryan, sometimes known as the Poet Laureate of the South, and John Banister Tabb, another popular Southern poet. Virginia poet George Dillon won the Pulitzer Prize for poetry in 1932.

William Cabell Bruce was awarded the Pulitzer Prize for biography in 1918 with his work on Benjamin Franklin.

Willa Cather, born in Winchester, Ellen Glasgow, John Warwick Daniel, author of the *Lame Lion of Lynchburg*, Mary Johnston, Francis Parkinson Keyes, born at Charlottesville, and James Branch Cabell are other well-known Virginia writers.

Such Interesting People

On a list of the household "goods" owned by planter Jones Burroughs is a notation, "One Negro boy, 'Booker,' value $400.00." As that little boy grew up and became Booker T. Washington, no one could possibly measure in dollars his value to all mankind.

He had been given his name Booker because he had loved books almost from his earliest days. After emancipation he went with his mother to West Virginia, where he worked in a salt furnace and also a coal mine, but he kept up his school work and later was graduated from Hampton Institute, where he worked as a janitor to earn his board. He then taught and studied at Wayland Seminary in Washington, D.C. He was given a faculty position at Hampton Institute. His success there led to his being asked to organize the Normal and Industrial Institute for Negroes at Tuskegee, Alabama. His work at Tuskegee has given him rank as one of the leading American educators of all time.

His biography is one of the best known of all such works—*Up From Slavery.*

Other prominent Virginia Negroes include Dr. James Solomon Russell, born a slave, founder of St. Paul's Normal and Industrial School for Negroes at Lawrenceville; James H. Holmes of the First African Baptist Church, with 5,000 members; Dr. Daniel Norton, Robert Norton, James Bland, and Dr. Thomas Bayne, Negro leaders after the emancipation. Of Dr. Bayne, a dentist, it was said that he was "one of

BOOKER T. WASHINGTON

the shrewdest politicians of his day, whose ready tongue enabled him easily to turn aside the ridicule that met any Negro representative who rose to speak."

When the Richmond Theater burned in 1811, an heroic slave, Gilbert Hunt, saved 20 women and children by catching them in his arms as they were thrown from upper windows to escape the flames. A devoted Negro gravedigger, remembered only as "Yellow Fever Jack," was the hero of the awful Norfolk yellow fever epidemic of 1855. A monument in a Norfolk cemetery remembers his faithfulness.

There were also Virginia heroines. Molly Tynes made a 40-mile, Paul Revere-type ride across the countryside to warn of a coming Union attack. On the other side was Elizabeth Van Lew, who risked her life at Richmond as a Union agent. Outstanding among war heroines was Sally Tompkins, in charge of a Confederate hospital, who was raised to the rank of captain in the Confederate army.

Virginia heroes of the Revolution were many. Among those who are not so well-known were General John Cropper who, single-handed, drove off an entire British raiding party near Accomac, and Peter Francisco, who fought an entire brigade by himself and was known as Virginia's Hercules. He was so strong that he was said to have tossed a man clear onto the roof of a house, and on another occasion he threw a horse over a fence.

The Reverend John Muhlenburg supported the Revolution enthusiastically. In 1774 he drafted a freedom resolution, and in January 1776 he preached a sermon on the text: "There is a time to every purpose . . . a time to war, and a time to peace." At the height of his dramatic address, the minister threw off his robes and stood in the uniform of a colonel in the Revolutionary army.

Another little-known but valiant patriot was Colonel Richard W. R. F. Lewis, brother-in-law of George Washington. Colonel Lewis completely outfitted three entire regiments of troops wholly at his own expense. He even presented a ship to the "Virginia Navy." His contributions to the cause were so great that he died in debt.

Other unusual Virginians include John Lynch, the Quaker who founded Lynchburg when he was only 17 years old; his brother Charles Lynch, whose harsh treatment of Tories and criminals during the Revo-

lution gave his name to the term Lynch law; Totopotomoi, Chief of the Pamunkey Indians, who gave his life fighting to defend the colonists; John Randolph of Roanoke, eccentric public figure who asked when he died to be buried facing west so he could watch Henry Clay; "Mad" Ann Bailey, who avenged the death of her husband by a long career as scout, spy, messenger and Indian hunter, who killed untold numbers of Indians and lived to the age of 83; and Grace Sherwood, one of two Virginia women tried for witchcraft.

One of the best-known women of her time was Nancy Langhorne, born in Danville. She married Viscount Waldorf Astor, and as Lady Astor became a powerful British politician, the first woman ever to sit in the British Parliament.

Another Virginian of an earlier time who made an impression when he visited in England was William Byrd II, (known as the Black Swan), of the prominent and wealthy Byrd family. The elegance and flair of this man from the "wilderness" created much astonishment and admiration in British society. An amusing story is told that when Byrd gave land for a new church in Virginia he contributed a plot a long way from his splendid Westover Plantation. He explained that if the church were nearby he would be expected to entertain the whole congregation for dinner every Sunday after church.

Three prominent entertainers were born in Virginia. Singer Kate Smith was a native of Greenville; Francis Xavier Bushman, one of the first great movie stars, who appeared in 402 films, was born in Norfolk; famed and much-loved Negro entertainer Bill "Bojangles" Robinson was born in Richmond.

Finally, all "in-laws" may take heart from the example of Sarah Winston Henry, mother of Patrick Henry. This noble woman was admired by all. Her son-in-law Colonel Samuel Meredith held her in such esteem that he asked to be buried at her feet—surely the highest possible praise.

Collecting Your Thoughts

Probably Virginia has produced more prominent public figures than any other state; is there any explanation for this?

64

Teaching and Learning

As early as 1618 the people of Virginia had chartered "the college and university of Virginia" at Henricopolis, making it the first college to be chartered in the present United States. However, after Henricopolis was destroyed in the massacre of 1622, plans for the University of Henrico were laid aside. The idea of a college was revived when in 1693 their majesties William and Mary granted a charter for a college at Williamsburg to bear their names. James Blair, who had gone to England to rouse interest in such a college, came back to Williamsburg bearing the charter along with an endowment from the crown and private parties, and a plan by England's greatest architect, Christopher Wren, for the principal building.

In 1694 the college received the only coat of arms ever granted an American college. As payment for its 20,000 acres of endowed land, the college is still supposed to pay to the governor each year two copies of Latin verse. Included in the college's endowment, also, is 300 pounds donated by several pirates. In 1776 America's best-known honorary scholastic society, Phi Beta Kappa, was founded at William and Mary; George Washington was made chancellor in 1788.

CHRISTOPHER WREN BUILDING
WILLIAM AND MARY COLLEGE

ROTUNDA, UNIVERSITY OF
VIRGINIA LIBRARY

Although the College of William and Mary was the second to be founded in the United States (after Harvard), it has not had continuous operation. It suspended its operations in the wartime years from 1861 to 1865 and was closed from 1881 to 1889. One of America's leading educators, Dr. Lyon Gardiner Tyler, reopened the college in 1889 and served as its president for 31 years. In 1906 the College of William and Mary came under state control.

Among the many distinguished persons educated at William and Mary were three Presidents: Jefferson, Monroe and Tyler. The college established America's first teaching in political economy in 1784, and the first school of history in 1803.

Education was one of Thomas Jefferson's greatest interests. He said "I look to the diffusion of light and education as the resource most to be relied on for ameliorating the condition, promoting the virtue and advancing the happiness of man." As early as 1779 Jefferson had introduced a bill to create a university, but it was not until after he retired as President that he was able to get a bill passed in 1818 to begin a state university. Through Jefferson's persuasion, this was started at Central College, which had been established two years earlier at Charlottesville. University of Virginia classes began in 1825 with 40 students and 7 faculty members.

The unusual official name of the University was and still is "The Rector and Visitors of the University of Virginia." Jefferson became the first rector and was the guiding genius of the university until his death, designing its buildings, its serpentine brick fences and its spacious lawns and "ranges." This was the first higher education institution in America to be separated from church influence. Jefferson had said, "The institution will be based on the illimitable freedom of the human mind. For here we are not afraid to follow the truth wherever it may lead or to tolerate any error so long as reason is left free to combat it."

Jefferson insisted that the narrow curriculum of other American colleges be broadened, and the university was the first to offer music and other more liberal subjects. Students and faculty were given wide freedom; an honor system was established, and students who broke their pledge of honor were dismissed. It may seem strange to many that at such a school women students were not admitted until 1920.

The University of Virginia has never closed, although only a few students attended between 1861 and 1865, and many of the buildings were used as wartime hospitals. Among the many famous graduates have been Edgar Allan Poe and Woodrow Wilson. Following a rule laid down by Jefferson, the university has never granted an honorary degree.

Today the University of Virginia enrolls 17,000 students.

Another prominent "double-name" university in Virginia is Washington and Lee at Lexington. This was founded as Augusta Academy in 1749 and then known as Liberty Hall, until George Washington donated 200 shares of James River Canal Company Stock; then it changed its name to Washington. When Robert E. Lee became its head in 1865, it added his name.

Another famed Lexington institution is Virginia Military Institute, one of the best known of its type in the country. One of its most famous "Rats" (first year students) was George Catlett Marshall, later to become General of the Army, Secretary of Defense and Secretary of State. Stonewall Jackson was a faculty member, and the institute still proudly remembers the gallant charge of its boy cadets who tipped the balance of battle at New Market in 1864.

Virginia Polytechnic Institute at Blacksburg is another technical school of great renown. It is often ranked among the top ten engineering schools of the nation. One of its most unusual divisions is the highly regarded Food Processing Laboratory.

Hampton Institute grew out of the desire of emancipated Negroes for education, and it expanded rapidly to become one of the most highly regarded institutions of its kind. The tours of its Hampton Singers have added to its world-wide fame.

Among the best-known colleges for women are Sweet Briar College, Amherst, and Randolph Macon College. Randolph Macon College was opened in 1830 and moved to Ashland in 1868. It was the first Methodist

Episcopal Church college to be established in the United States. The college for women was established at Lynchburg in 1893. Nobel Prize winning author Pearl Buck is one of its most distinguished graduates.

The 57 institutions of higher education in Virginia enrolled 81,000 students in 1965. Prominent among these institutions are the University of Richmond; Virginia Union University, also at Richmond; Old Dominion College, Norfolk, now one of the largest in the state; and Virginia State College, Petersburg.

One of Virginia's early distinguished educators was George Wythe, America's first law professor, who taught John Marshall, Thomas Jefferson, James Monroe and Henry Clay. His strange death came when he was poisoned by a nephew who was impatient to inherit his uncle's estate.

Virginia lawmakers have shown an interest in education from the beginning. The first discussion in the House of Burgesses was concerned with education. In the will of Benjamin Syms in 1634, 200 acres and 8 cows were left to create a school. This became the first free school and the first school with an endowment in all the colonies. The school still operates today as Syms-Eaton Academy at Hampton.

Thomas Jefferson was the first leading figure in favor of free education for all children. It was not until 1870, however, that Virginia had started on a program of providing such education. In 1905 a popular campaign led to better schools, including high schools as well as colleges for teachers.

Much of Virginia's great improvement in education has come after the close of World War II. Fifty per cent of all schools now in use have been built since 1950.

An unusual program of adult education is carried out in the Special Education Program. This provides training at state expense for those who would like to work in particular skilled occupations.

Collecting Your Thoughts

Many statistics help to understand the worth of schools in a state, such as the percentage of the people of the state who can read and write. See how many figures you can find on several aspects of education in Virginia, such as the amount spent for each pupil.

BLUE RIDGE MOUNTAINS

"Carry Me Back"

Visitors by the hundreds of thousands hearken to the Virginia state song and say to their travel agents, "Carry Me Back to Old Virginia." Each year tourists spend almost $300,000,000 in the state. Hardly anywhere will the visitor find more variety to claim his attention.

Almost nowhere else in all America is one surrounded by so much living history—the beginnings of our national traditions at Jamestown, the climax of two great wars, the estates and homes of probably more famous people than found anywhere else in the country, and all this charm of the older eras blending in with the newest and most up-to-date.

The sweep of scenery stretches from the quiet islands and sunny beaches past the picturesque villages and stirring cities to the crests of the mountains where America's most unique roads—Skyline Drive and Blue Ridge Parkway—literally carry the visitor over the "Mountain-Gabled Roof of Virginia" through the clouds past postcard vistas of beauty on every side and at every turn.

Here pastimes may include deep sea fishing quickly followed by the wonders of the depths of nine spectacular caverns, the attractions of vast national forests and state parks. Even the unexpected fun of skiing in the highlands on man-made snow has been added to Virginia's lure.

Innumerable museums, battlefield parks, nine resident symphony orchestras and other cultural attractions also may be found.

Not the least attractive is the long tradition of good food in Virginia—home of mouth-watering Virginia hams and delicate spoon bread, deviled crab and plump Virginia oysters, on the half shell or roasted and dripping with melted butter, and many other native dishes perfected over the generations.

No wonder that more and more people are discovering that they really mean it when they sing "Carry Me Back—."

Vibrant Past, Vibrant Future—Richmond

The statues of Stonewall Jackson and other Confederate heroes line Richmond's magnificent Monument Avenue. Statues of those who died fighting face defiantly north; those who returned face the South and home. Something of the same is true of the city itself; few cities can look to a more inspiring past while at the same time facing an exciting future.

In 1607, the year of Jamestown's founding, an exploring party set up a cross not far from the spot where Richmond's great north-south expressway now strides across the James River on stilts of steel and concrete. In 1644 the spot became a frontier fort. Ninety years later, William Byrd II set aside a tiny part of his vast domain to become a town site, and in 1737, Major William Mayo laid out the first streets and named the new town Richmond.

During the Revolution, Richmond became a target for Tory raiders under traitor Benedict Arnold. When the state government had to flee the British invaders in 1779, the straggling village suddenly found itself the heir to the capital long held by aristocratic Williamsburg.

During another war for four tense and drama-packed years, Richmond stood not only as the capital of Virginia but as the capital of the fated Confederacy. Fortunately, the flames which its own people set to keep it from falling into northern hands spared much of its historic architecture.

Saved was the priceless capitol building, designed by Thomas Jefferson. Part of his plan for this classic building was based on the design of the ancient temple built by the Romans at Nimes, France. It may have been the first modern building to follow the architecture of the ancient masters. Here the New World's oldest continuous legislative assembly still meets; here Aaron Burr was tried for treason; here Virginia approved the Articles of Secession, and here the Confederate Congress held its momentous meetings. The original section of the capitol was finished in 1792. Additions were made in 1904 and 1905.

Renowned early American architect Robert Mills wrote of the capitol, "I remember the impression it made on my mind when first I came in view of it coming from the South. It gave me an idea of the effect of those Greek temples which are the admiration of the world."

In the center of the capitol rotunda is the only statue ever created of George Washington as he actually looked in life. Famed sculptor Jean Antoine Houdon followed Washington on his rounds of Mount Vernon until one day Washington began to argue with a salesman about the price of a plow. The gestures of this homespun incident are preserved for posterity in Houdon's remarkable statue. Here is the only truthful answer to the question, "How did Washington really look?"

Also in the capitol is the original plaster model of the capitol building which Jefferson had made and sent home from France.

Outside is the equestrian statue of Washington by Thomas Crawford, cast in Munich at a cost of $100,000. Also in the capitol complex is the Governor's Mansion, 1813, and the Virginia State Museum, in the Finance Building.

Few places in American history hold the thrill for visitors as the spot where Patrick Henry thundered forth his call for liberty or death in St. John's Church. Another historic spot is the White House of the Confederacy, wartime home of Jefferson Davis. From the porch Davis' son, Joseph Davis, fell accidentally to his untimely death. Today the building houses what is said to be the largest collection anywhere of mementoes of the Civil War.

Other war memorials are the mighty Memorial Carillon in Byrd Park to the memory of Virginia's doughboys of World War I, and the unique colonnaded marble structure high above the James River where are inscribed the names of the Virginia men and women who gave their lives in the struggles of World War II and Korea.

Richmond's oldest house now is a shrine to Edgar Allan Poe. Other interesting homes are the John Marshall House, Virginia House, and Wilton. Famed plantations near the city include Sherwood Forest, home of John Tyler, and Berkeley, birthplace of William Henry Harrison. It is interesting that this mansion was also the birthplace of the familiar wartime bugle call "Taps."

One of the country's most impressive and progressive art museums is the Virginia Museum of Fine Arts, established in 1936 as the first state museum. The museum created a new type of "dynamic" display—the Artmobile, galleries on wheels that carry priceless exhibits of art to areas not served by the state's network of 51 associate museums—a unique project now being copied by museums all over the world. The museum also has a notable $1,000,000 Theater of the Performing Arts.

The museum is now embarking on a bold $5,600,000 expansion program financed by state appropriation, probably the most significant state contribution to fine art in the nation. New construction will include a breathtaking entrance portico and waterfall flanked by sculpture gardens. It is interesting to note that most significant cultural organizations throughout Virginia receive state funds for museum, symphonic, art and other purposes.

Other Richmond museums are the Valentine Museum, Virginia Civil War Centennial Center, Richmond Academy of Medicine, and Battle Abbey.

In the vicinity of Richmond are many interesting attractions for visitors. Petersburg, about 25 miles to the south, is a fascinating center. Here is where George Washington actually told a lie, and wrote about it in his own words: "Having suffered very much by the dust yesterday, and finding that parties of Horse, and a number of other Gentlemen were intending to attend me part of the way to day, I caused their enquiries respecting the time of my setting out, to be answered that, I should endeavor to do it before eight o'clock; but did it a little after five." It was at Petersburg that the mayor is said to have been the first person to bestow on Washington the title "Father of His Country."

At Petersburg are memories of its pillaging in the Revolution and the key role played by the city in 1864 and 1865. At Petersburg National Military Park the "Dictator" can still be seen; this was the mightiest siege mortar of the war. Here may be seen the remains of one of the most fantastic actions of the war. A regiment of miners from Pennsylvania burrowed under the Confederate lines for 500 feet. In this tunnel 8,000 pounds of gunpowder set off an explosion which stunned both sides and killed many Confederate soldiers, blowing a crater 30 feet deep stretching for 135 feet. Federal forces were driven into the pit and virtually massacred. The defeat may have been a key reason in the Union failure to take Richmond in 1864.

Other historic spots near Richmond are Studley House, birthplace of Patrick Henry, Seven Pines National Cemetery and the little brick schoolhouse where boyish Thomas Jefferson received some of his early education. True to the spirit of boyish pranks, he inscribed his name on the wall.

POE MUSEUM
OLDEST HOUSE
IN RICHMOND

"Three Significant Places"

Williamsburg, Jamestown and Yorktown, all on a small peninsula of land between the James and the York rivers, have been described as "the three most significant places in our heritage."

They rest quietly now, those pioneer colonists; the ancient trees have wrapped themselves around their tombs; only a vine-covered church tower remains as a reminder of all their accomplishments; even their island itself would have been washed away if it had not been for a sea wall built in 1901. The rest of the earliest portion of Jamestown consists of only a fragment of a foundation, the remnant of a street, ancient hedgerow or property ditch, or some other scattered relics.

In spite of the fact, however, that almost all traces of the settlement are gone, an ever-increasing flood of visitors comes, paying tribute to the fact that here was the planting, growth and flowering of the miracle of American colonization.

The area is now Jamestown Colonial National Historical Park. The ruined church remains, with three-foot-thick broken walls of handmade brick, those of the structure built in 1639 on the spot where John Rolfe and Pocahontas were married. The actual earrings worn by the Indian princess may still be seen in the Visitor Center of the national park, along with other relics and exhibits of colonial times. America's first manufacturing operation has been reproduced in the Glass House, where glassware is made just as it was in 1608. Five-mile wilderness trail through the forests provides a vivid example of what the region was like when the colonists first came.

Nearby, the Commonwealth of Virginia has built a fascinating reproduction of earlier days, called Jamestown Festival Park. Here is a fascinating full-scale reconstruction of triangular James Fort and its 18 wattle and daub buildings, thrown up in 1607 to guard against Indians and Spaniards. There are displays in a New World pavilion and an Old World pavilion, and a reconstruction of Powhatan's lodge. Full-scale reproductions of the three tiny ships, *Susan Constant* (100 tons), *Godspeed* (40 tons) and *Discovery* (20 tons) cause visitors to marvel constantly that people were willing to risk their lives and cross the mighty ocean in such tiny vessels.

As Christmas approaches in Williamsburg, the great yule log is brought in. Carolers in colonial costume stroll from window to window with their message of song. The traditional Christmas guns are fired. The governor himself invites visitors to a Christmas harpsichord concert in the candlelit hall of the magnificent Governor's Mansion. Feasts of Virginia ham, Sally Lunn bread, roasted Virginia oysters, fragrant mince pies and flaming plum pudding weigh down the groaning boards, and those who feast, carefully tie yard-square napkins about their necks. Craftsmen in 11 different shops hurry to finish their work in hand printing, blacksmithing, wigmaking, hand leather tooling or candle making in time for Christmas. Coachmen in tricornered hats guide their horses down Duke of Gloucester Street.

All this is as it took place in seventeenth century America. Nowhere else in the world is it possible to go back so completely and authentically to another world as in Colonial Williamsburg.

This amazing accomplishment has cost almost $77,000,000 and more than a generation of extremely painstaking work of hundreds of experts as well as the devotion of people great and small to make the unusual dream come true. The dream was that of the Reverend Dr. W. A. R. Goodwin, who fired the imagination of John D. Rockefeller, Jr., who saw in it a great educational project with the aim "that the future may learn from the past."

Today's visitor may see most of Williamsburg as it looked at its peak as the fashionable social capital of America. Thirty-seven buildings, containing 230 exhibition rooms, may now be seen just as they once looked. Some were still standing when the restoration began, others such as the historic Governor's Mansion (burned during its use as a Revolutionary hospital) had to be carefully rebuilt on the original foundations.

To restore the mansion, an old picture was carefully studied as were 300 pages of original materials on the building. Complete inventories of the contents of the building under three different governors were available in order to refurnish the mansion almost exactly as it was in its glory. The superb gardens, including the vast maze, have been carefully recreated.

The splendid capitol building has been called "best and most commodius pile in Colonial America." On a candlelight tour of the rebuilt structure many visitors have the eerie feeling that they have been transported backward into an earlier era.

The old jail was still standing, and was simply restored. Here the infamous pirate Blackbeard was once held, and nine of his pirate crew were executed on Gallows Road.

Fascinating, too, at Williamsburg are the colonial craft shops; milling, spinning and weaving, millinery, bakery, apothecary, bootmaking and many others. In these, workers ply their trades just as in the old days, along Duke of Gloucester Street, sometimes called "the most historic street in all America."

Other interesting portions of Williamsburg are the Abby Aldrich Rockefeller Folk Art Collection, the Craft House, and the historic College of William and Mary, with its Wren Building, oldest academic building in the United States.

Jamestown and Williamsburg are connected by the Colonial Parkway, which also ties in the third historic site included in the Colonial National Historical Park—Yorktown. The town itself is almost surrounded by Yorktown Battlefield, where the remains of British fortifications and the camping places of the Americans may still be seen. The Visitor Center has many interesting exhibits of the Revolution. A tour of the battleground may include the headquarter locations of von Steuben, Lafayette, Rochambeau and Washington. On the edge of the battlefield is Moore House where the Articles of Capitulation were written. Yorktown National Cemetery contains the graves of 2,204 American dead.

MOORE HOUSE

Four for the Roads

The metropolitan area centered at Hampton Roads includes four major Virginia communities—Norfolk, Portsmouth, Newport News and Hampton.

Norfolk is now the largest city in Virginia and completely modern, with one of the most complete civic centers in the country, including a new $9,000,000 city hall. However, the influence of the sea and of its long history still are strong.

Old St. Paul's Church was one of the few buildings to survive the battles of 1776; in its aged walls may still be seen the cannonballs embedded during the British cannonades in the War of 1812. The Adam Thoroughgood House is believed to be the oldest English-built brick residence in the nation.

One of the newest shrines for visitors in Norfolk is the General Douglas MacArthur Memorial, housed in what once was the city hall. Here is one of the world's finest collections of war materials of this century as well as the tomb of one of America's most famous generals, whose memory certainly will not "fade away" in Norfolk, as he once poignantly predicted would happen to all "old soldiers."

Other interesting displays are to be seen at the Norfolk Museum; magnificent wood carvings and a fabulous oriental art collection are part of the collection of the Hermitage Foundation. At the Myers House visitors can enjoy the elegance of a home belonging to an eighteenth century merchant prince.

A special air-conditioned bus takes visitors on a guided tour of the world's greatest naval base and naval air station.

Norfolk is noted for its Gardens-by-the-Sea. Here in the spring 250,000 azaleas bloom, along with other spring blossoms, and a queen is crowned for the International Azalea Festival.

Summer playground of the area is famous Virginia Beach, with its two miles of boardwalk, eight miles of beach and fun in the surf.

Portsmouth is connected with Norfolk by two toll tunnels and two bridges. The Portsmouth section of the navy complex is known as Norfolk Naval Shipyard in Portsmouth. A Naval Shipyard Museum displays thousands of navy items, along with pictures and models of ships; at Portsmouth is the oldest naval hospital in the United States. Many notable historic homes may be visited in Portsmouth.

Near Portsmouth is the Dismal Swamp, once the eerie refuge of desperate fugitives; boat tours through this unusual area may be arranged.

Newport News, named for Sir Christopher Newport, is the third of the great cities on Hampton Roads. It is noted for two unique museums. The Mariners Museum is surrounded by an 880-acre game sanctuary; in the museum are vast collections of ship models and miniature ships, ships instruments and other exhibits. One of the most fascinating displays is that of the figureheads from many ships, ranging from saucy mermaids to the prim figure of a captain's wife with parasol and prayer book. A huge golden eagle figurehead spreads his wings across most of a room.

The War Memorial Museum of Virginia holds one of the most complete collections of materials on World Wars I and II and Korea. Relic of other wars, Fort Monroe frowns out over the entrance to Chesapeake Bay and Hampton Roads. Famous prisoners held over the years at Fort Monroe included unfortunate Chief Black Hawk and Jefferson Davis.

Hampton, begun in 1610, is the fourth major city in the Norfolk metropolitan area. Because Jamestown is not now occupied, Norfolk claims to be the oldest continuously inhabited English settlement in the New World. Syms-Eaton Museum at Hampton honors the names of the men who started the first free schools in America—Benjamin Syms and Thomas Eaton; here are Indian relics and mementoes of old Hampton. Hampton Institute, Langley Air Force Base, National Aeronautics and Space Administration and Big Bethel Battlefield are other points of interest in the Hampton area.

The Rest of the East

Fairfax County is one of the largest areas in the country under a single local government. The biggest city in the Virginia portion of the Washington, D.C., metropolitan area is Alexandria, begun in 1732 by a group of Scottish merchants. George Washington helped to survey the streets.

Washington is remembered by his fellow Masons in the George Washington Masonic National Memorial at Alexandria. This startling 333 foot high building with carillon and organ was built at a cost of

$5,000,000 with contributions from 3,000,000 Masons all over the country.

Three wars all spared Alexandria, so that homes of many famous people are still to be seen there. One of the most unusual houses was the thin "Flounder" house, built that way to avoid taxes. In Christ Church is the brass and crystal chandelier presented by vestryman George Washington. On the streets of Alexandria the visitor can still buy the *Gazette,* oldest daily in the country. Here also is the old apothecary shop where Martha Washington bought castor oil by the quart.

There are no incorporated cities or towns in Arlington County, but its population is about 170,000, and within its boundaries are some of the nation's most historic sites, as well as the vast Pentagon Building, largest office building in the world, and Washington National Airport.

Arlington National Cemetery is the largest and best known of all our national cemeteries, where more than 119,000 are buried. Among the most famous of those who rest in Arlington are Presidents John F. Kennedy and William Howard Taft. Other famous names include General John J. Pershing, who lies among his men at his own request in a less prominent part of the cemetery, Robert Todd Lincoln, William Jennings Bryan, Admirals Robert E. Perry and Richard E. Byrd, General George C. Marshall, and John Foster Dulles.

Pierre Charles L'Enfant, designer of Washington, is buried in a grave overlooking the city. Polish patriot-musician Jan Paderewski is buried temporarily in Arlington. The Arlington Monument to the Confederate Dead was a gift of the Daughters of the Confederacy to symbolize a reunited people. The mast of the Battleship *Maine* stands on high ground, a memorial to the men who lost their lives when it was sunk.

The Arlington Memorial Amphitheater, dedicated by Woodrow Wilson in 1920, was built as a memorial to the Army, Navy and Marine Corps dead and as a gathering place for those who attend Memorial Day and other services.

Nearby is one of America's most hallowed shrines—the tomb of the unknowns. Great pains were taken to be sure that the hero buried beneath the simple impressive monument was truly "known but to God." The body was placed in its present resting place after being brought from Washington in one of the most celebrity-filled processions of all

HERE RESTS IN
HONORED GLORY
AN AMERICAN
SOLDIER
KNOWN BUT TO GOD

time. In 1958 two more bodies were added to the shrine, one to represent the unknown dead of World War II, the other to represent those of the Korean War.

In the cemetery area is Custis-Lee Mansion National Memorial. When General Lafayette visited here in 1824 he said the view was unequaled in all the world. The stately house overlooking Washington was built by George Washington's foster son, Martha's grandson, George Washington Parke Custis, whose daughter married Robert E. Lee. The beautiful interior now has many mementoes of the Washington and Lee families.

An even more famous mansion is Mount Vernon, the estate so beloved by George Washington. In 1853 Ann Pamela Cunningham organized the Mount Vernon Ladies' Association of the Union to buy and restore the historic house and grounds. Today it is much as it was in Washington's day and is considered to be a good expression of his character. In spite of his tremendous public works, it might be said that Mount Vernon and his family were Washington's principal interest. Some of the happiest pages from his diary centered about the plantation life here that he loved. Among the interesting contents of the home are the harpsichord Washington imported for his stepdaughter, Nelly, at a cost of 1,000 pounds, most of his books, and the key to the Bastille presented by Lafayette.

George and Martha Washington are buried in a simple tomb on the grounds, spurning the elaborate tomb prepared for them in the national capitol building. Thirty-one other members of the Washington family are buried in the cemetery at George Washington Birthplace National Monument near Oak Grove. The mansion in the monument is not the birthplace but a reproduction of a typical Virginia plantation.

Fredericksburg has some of the finest homes left from colonial times, including Mary Washington's house, where she gave her blessing to her son before he went to the Presidency, and Kenmore, often called one of the best restorations in the country. At Fredericksburg is the law office of James Monroe, now a museum where may be seen the desk on which the President wrote the Monroe Doctrine.

Fredericksburg and Spotsylvania National Military Park commemorate some of the heaviest fighting ever experienced on the continent. The park includes portions of four battlefields and the Fredericksburg National Cemetery. Almost 13,000 of those buried there were unknown. Nearby is the Stonewall Jackson Memorial Shrine, at the plantation office where Jackson died of pneumonia after being wounded. It was here that he murmured while dying, "Let us cross over the river, and rest under the shade of the trees."

The Indians called Virginia's lower peninsula Accawmacke; today one of its counties is Accomack, taken from the Indian name. The picturesque eastern shore is said to be a "world apart." One of the most exciting events of the region is the annual Pony Penning Day. Wild horses have lived so long on the not very nutritious grasses of Chincoteague Island that they are now stunted to slightly more than pony size. Each year they are rounded up, forced to swim the inlet, foals are branded, and many ponies auctioned. Chincoteague Ocean Beach on Assateague Island is a part of the National Seashore.

On the eastern shore may be seen many houses built in the 1600's and early 1700's. Tangier Island, in the middle of lower Chesapeake Bay, has about 1,000 inhabitants who speak with an old-English accent and follow many customs of their ancestors. The streets of Tangier are not wide enough for automobiles.

Four Interior Cities

Roanoke, first settled in 1740, is the leading commercial and industrial center of western Virginia—a manufacturer of fabricated steel, railroad cars, electronic equipment, glass fiber boats, fabrics, clothing, wood furniture and flour. It lies in a cup-shaped area between the Allegheny Mountains and the Blue Ridge.

Rising 1,000 feet within the city is Mill Mountain, topped by Roanoke's famous neon star, said to be the largest in the world. The city-owned mountain, with magnificent view, is a park with the only Children's Zoo in the state.

Roanoke's Transportation Museum displays a collection of boats, locomotives, airplanes and antique cars.

Near Roanoke is Booker T. Washington National Monument. On the 200-acre plantation where the Negro leader was born as a slave is a replica of his boyhood cabin. The spring from which the family took its water still flows. The Visitor Center has exhibits showing Washington's life.

The tobacco town of Lynchburg perches on the bluffs of the James River. It boasts the largest dark tobacco market in the South, one of the largest anywhere, where the strange chant of the tobacco auctioneer rings out. The town was founded by a 17-year-old Quaker, John Lynch, in 1757. The striking Lynchburg War Memorial looks out over the city and is reached by an impressive approach of stairs and terraces. At nearby Brookneal is the simple tomb of Patrick Henry on the grounds of his last home, Red Hill.

Even today Charlottesville seems to be dominated by memories of its most famous citizen, Thomas Jefferson—the estate he created, the university he founded and designed.

The university, with its handsome red brick buildings, sweeping vistas and serpentine walls, one brick thick, another Jefferson innovation, and its ancient trees, has long been one of the most admired campuses in America. Its Brooks Museum offers interesting displays, and the university rooms occupied by Woodrow Wilson and Edgar Allan Poe as students are open to the public.

The Thomas Jefferson Memorial Foundation has restored and maintains Monticello, the estate built by Jefferson with materials made on the spot, even its nails. The inventions and devices Jefferson installed in the interior make it one of the unique houses of America. Shadwell, Jefferson's birthplace near Monticello, has been reconstructed.

Ash Lawn, home of another President, James Monroe, is also open to the public and it contains many of Monroe's possessions.

Charlottesville is noted for its many monuments, including those of Stonewall Jackson on his horse Little Sorrell, Robert E. Lee, and Lewis and Clark. There is also a George Rogers Clark Memorial.

At Barboursville, in Madison Cemetery, are the graves of James and Dolly Madison.

Woodrow Wilson's birthplace is now a national shrine at Staunton. A different kind of "shrine" is the McCormick Reaper Museum, where the first reaper is displayed. General U. S. Grant allowed the Staunton Military Band to keep their instruments at the end of the war. When he came South as President, the band gave him the first welcome he had ever received in the South. Near Staunton is a unique formation known as Natural Chimneys. Here an unusual jousting tournament is held. This is said to be America's oldest sporting event.

The Mountain Sweep

Two of the world's most unusual roads snake their way along the crests of the Blue Ridge—the Blue Ridge Parkway and connecting Skyline Drive. About 300 square miles of the most beautiful scenery of the Blue Ridge is found in Shenandoah National Park—still a wonderful, unspoiled wilderness playground. Shenandoah Valley has been called "Virginia's valley of wonders, where both nature and man have carved boldly,—" a vast fertile checkerboard of green and gold.

Natural wonders of the region include famed Luray Caverns and Shenandoah Caverns. Another wonder, farther to the south, is Natural Bridge. Thomas Jefferson bought the bridge for 20 shillings, and millions of visitors from all over the world have come ever since to marvel at it. An impressive program of music and lights adds to the interest of the attraction.

NATURAL BRIDGE

The oldest Virginia city west of the Blue Ridge is Winchester, sometimes known as the Apple Capital of the World. Here was George Washington's first office and wartime headquarters of General Jackson and later of General Sheridan.

Two of the most famous comrades in arms have found their final resting place at Lexington. Robert E. Lee's grave lies beneath the chapel of Washington and Lee University, under the famous recumbent statue of the General. A bronze statue marks the grave of Stonewall Jackson in the Presbyterian Cemetery. The only home he ever owned is now restored as a memorial to him.

The Museum of Virginia Military Institute at Lexington has many mementoes of war and of wartime figures, including Jackson, Marshall and George S. Patton.

Covington is surrounded by Warm Springs, Sweet Springs and Lick mountains. Thomas Jefferson once described nearby Falling Springs as "the only remarkable cascade in this country . . . it falls over a rock 200 feet into the valley. This cataract will bear no comparison with that of Niagara, as to the quantity of water . . . but it is half as high again."

One of the attractions of Covington is a humpback covered bridge, the only one of this construction remaining in the country. Crow Tavern at Covington once overflowed with so many travelers that the tavern rules prohibited more than five persons in a bed. Warm meals were advertised at $12\frac{2}{3}$ cents and cold ones at $10\frac{1}{2}$ cents each.

New Castle was noted for its fair. In 1737 the sponsors of the fair announced "that 20 horses or mares do run round a three-mile course for a prize of five pounds . . . that a violin be played for by 20 fiddlers . . . they are all to play together and each a different tune . . . that handsome entertainment be provided for the subscribers and their wives; and such of them as are not so happy as to have wives may treat any other lady . . . that a quire of ballads be sung by a number of songsters, all of them to have liquor sufficient to clear their wind pipes."

Radford was the gateway to the Virginia highlands and New River Valley. Here Mary Draper Ingles made one of the most famous of all escapes from Indian captivity. Here also the Ingles Ferry provided a link in the Great Road from Philadelphia to Louisville. Radford arsenal manufactured powder for the Revolutionary War.

Best known of all Virginia stage activities is world-famous Barter Theater at Abingdon. It was founded by a group of Broadway actors during the depression. Theater-goers without money could bring a glass of jelly, ham or other worthwhile item to barter for a ticket. Today the Barter Theater is the Virginia State Theater—only state theater in the country.

Bristol, Virginia, is one of a pair of twin cities on the Virginia-Tennessee line, which runs down the middle of State Street. Bristol is now a principal industrial center. Interesting Bristol Caverns are nearby, as are South Holston Dam and Lake.

West of Gate City is an unusual natural tunnel 100 feet in diameter and 900 feet long, carved through the rock by wind and water. It is used as a railroad tunnel and described as the "oldest railroad tunnel in the world."

Big Stone Gap is the home of Southwest Virginia Museum, a collection of Indian relics, war mementoes, agricultural and other implements. The town still remembers the time its most famous son, author John Fox, Jr., married famed light opera star Fritzi Scheff after a 24-hour courtship and brought her home to Big Stone Gap. The dazzling, bejeweled favorite of two continents found the hills not as romantic as her husband had written about them and soon left both them and him.

Breaks Interstate Park in the Cumberlands, shared with Kentucky and Cumberland Gap National Historic Park preserve some of America's most historic wilderness area. Through this region came some of the earliest western pioneers. Through them Virginia became the "Mother of the Frontier," as well as the "Mother of English Settlement in America."

Instant Facts

Became 10th state, June 25, 1788
Capital—Richmond, founded 1737
State Motto—Sic Semper Tyrannis (Thus always to tyrants)
Familiar Name—Old Dominion
State Bird—Cardinal
State Dog—Foxhound
State Flower and State Tree—American dogwood
State Song—*Carry Me Back to Old Virginia,* by James A. Bland
Area—40,815 square miles
Greatest Length (north to south)—209 miles
Greatest Width (east to west)—452 miles
Highest Point—5,729 feet (Mount Rogers)
Lowest Point—Sea Level
Geographic Center—Buckingham
Highest Recorded Temperature—110° (Balcony Falls)
Lowest Recorded Temperature—minus 29° (Monterey)
Population—4,456,000 (1965 estimate)
Population Density—99.6 persons per square mile (1960 census)
Principal Cities—Norfolk

Norfolk	304,869	(1960 census)
Richmond	219,958	
Portsmouth	144,773	
Newport News	113,662	
Roanoke	97,110	
Alexandria	91,023	

You Have a Date with History

1497—Cabot's exploration, basis of British claims to region
1607—London Company colonists found Virginia
1608—Glass plant at Jamestown is first American manufacturing concern
1609—John Smith returns to England
1610—Starving time relieved; Hampton founded
1614—John Rolfe plants tobacco, marries Pocahontas
1618—Emperor Powhatan dies
1619—Oldest American legislature established
1622—Great massacre by Indians
1634—Benjamin Syms endows first free school in colonies
1674—Bacon's rebellion

1693—William and Mary College chartered
1699—Capital moved to Williamsburg
1716—Governor Spotswood explores the West
1732—George Washington born
1736—Patrick Henry born
1737—Richmond founded
1743—Thomas Jefferson born at Shadwell
1751—James Madison born
1758—James Monroe born
1763—French and Indian War closes
1773—Virginia Committee of Correspondence set up; William Henry Harrison born
1776—Virginia declares itself a free state
1778—Slave trade forbidden in Virginia
1779—Richmond becomes Capital
1781—Cornwallis surrenders at Yorktown
1788—Statehood
1790—First canal in country opened—Richmond to Westham
1792—Original portion of Capitol completed; Kentucky separates
1799—George Washington and Patrick Henry die
1813—First steamboats in Virginia waters
1818—University of Virginia chartered
1826—Thomas Jefferson dies
1831—James Monroe dies; McCormick invents the reaper
1836—James Madison dies
1856—Thomas Woodrow Wilson born
1861—Virginia secedes
1862—Northern attacks repulsed
1863—Northern push again turned back; West Virginia separated
1865—Lee surrenders at Appomatox
1869—Reconstruction constitution approved
1870—Virginia again a sovereign state
1894—Boundary dispute with Maryland settled
1902—New state constitution "proclaimed"
1908—Saunton introduces city manager plan
1917—World War I begins, in which 91,623 from Virginia served
1924—Thomas Woodrow Wilson dies
1927—State government reorganized
1935—Shenandoah National Park established
1941—World War II begins, in which 214,903 from Virginia served
1966—State Department of Community Colleges established

Governors of the Commonwealth of Virginia

Patrick Henry, 1776–1779
Thomas Jefferson, 1779–1781
William Fleming, 1781
Thomas Nelson, Jr., 1781
Benjamin Harrison, 1781–1784
Patrick Henry, 1784–1786
Edmund Randolph, 1786–1788
Beverly Randolph, 1788–1791
Henry Lee, 1791–1794
Robert Brooke, 1794–1796
Hardin Burnley, 1796
James Wood, 1796–1799
J. Pendleton, 1799
James Monroe, 1799–1802
John Page, 1802–1805
William H. Cabell, 1805–1808
John Tyler, 1808–1811
George William Smith, 1811
James Monroe, 1811
Peyton Randolph, 1811–1812
James Barbour, 1812–1814
Wilson Cary Nicholas, 1814–1816
James Patton Preston, 1816–1819
Thomas Mann Randolph, 1819–1822
James Pleasants, Jr., 1822–1825
John Tyler, Jr., 1825–1827
William Branch Giles, 1827–1830
John Floyd, 1830–1834
Littleton Waller Tazewell, 1834–1836
Wyndham Robertson, 1836–1837
David Campbell, 1837–1840
Thomas Walker Gilmer, 1840–1841
John Mercer Patton, 1841
John Rutherford, 1841–1842
John Munford Gregory, 1843–1843
James McDowell, 1843–1846

William Smith, 1846–1849
John Buchanan Floyd, 1849–1852
Joseph Johnson, 1852–1856
Henry Alexander Wise, 1856–1860
John Letcher, 1860–1864
William Smith, 1864–1865
Francis Harrison Pierpont, 1865–1868
Henry Horatio Wells, 1868–1869
Gilbert Carlton Walker, 1869–1874
James Lawson Kemper, 1874–1878
Frederick William Mackey Holliday
    1878–1882
William Evelyn Cameron, 1882–1886
Fitzhugh Lee, 1886–1890
Philip Watkins McKinney, 1890–1894
Charles Triplett O'Ferrall, 1894–1898
James Hoge Tyler, 1898–1902
Andrew Jackson Montague, 1902–1906
Claude Augustus Swanson, 1906–1910
William Hodges Mann, 1910–1914
Henry Carter Stuart, 1914–1918
Westmoreland Davis, 1918–1922
Elbert Lee Trinkle, 1922–1926
Harry Flood Byrd, 1926–1930
John Garland Pollard, 1930–1934
George Campbell Perry, 1934–1938
James Hubert Price, 1938–1942
Colgate Whitehead Darden, Jr.,
    1942–1946
William Munford Tuck, 1946–1950
John Stewart Battle, 1950–1954
Thomas Bahnson Stanley, 1954–1958
James Lindsay Almond, Jr., 1958–1962
Albertis Sydney Harrison, Jr., 1962–1966
Mills E. Godwin, Jr., 1966–

Thinkers, Doers, Fighters

People of renown who have been associated with Virginia

Astor, Nancy Langhorne
Bacon, Nathaniel
Bassett, John David
Bruce, William Cabell
Burnett, Frances Hodgson
Bushman, Francis Xavier
Cabell, James Branch
Cather, Willa
Clark, George Rogers
Daniel, John Warwick
Glasgow, Ellen
Harrison, William Henry
Henry, Patrick
Huntington, Collis Porter
Jackson, Thomas Jonathan (Stonewall)
Jefferson, Thomas
Johnston, Mary
Keyes, Francis Parkinson
Lee, Henry (Lighthorse Harry)
Lee, Richard Henry
Lee, Robert Edward
Lee, Francis Lightfoot
Madison, Dorothea Payne (Dolly)
Madison, James
Marshall, George Catlett
Mason, George
McCormick, Cyrus Hall
Monroe, James
Poe, Edgar Allan
Powhatan, Emperor (Wahunsonacock)
Robinson, Bill (Bojangles)
Rolfe, John
Rolfe, Rebecca (Pocahontas)
Ryan, Abram Joseph
Scott, Winfield
Smith, John
Smith, Kate
Tabb, John Banister
Taylor, Zachary
Tyler, John
Washington, Booker Taliafero
Washington, George
Wilson, Thomas Woodrow

Annual Events

Jan-Feb—Antiques Forum, Williamsburg
March—Point to Point Races, Middleburg
March—Garden Symposium, Williamsburg
April—Shenandoah Apple Blossom Festival, Winchester
April—Historic Garden week, statewide, centered at Richmond
April—International Azalea Festival, Norfolk
April—Pilgrimage to Cape Henry, Portsmouth
April—Founders Day, Charlottesville
April—Homes Tour, Leesburg
April—Deep Run Hunt Race Meet, Richmond
April—Garden Club Tours, Portsmouth
April—Hunt Race Association, Middleburg

April—Garden Week, Fredericksburg
April—Dogwood Festival, Charlottesville
April-May—National Sports Car Races, Danville
April-May—Shenandoah Apple Blossom Festival, Winchester
June—Music Festival, Virginia Beach
June—Historic Homes Tour, Portsmouth
June—Horse Shows, Middleburg
June—Colonial Beach Water Festival, Fredericksburg
June—Music Festival, Virginia Beach
June—Hopewell Yacht Club Regatta, Hopewell
June—Horse Show, Wytheville
July—Boardwalk Art Show, Virginia Beach
July—Jazz Festival, Virginia Beach
July—Boardwalk Art Show, Portsmouth
July—Yacht Regattas, Hampton
July—Lotus Festival, Virginia Beach
July-August—Wild Pony Roundup and Penning Day, Chincoteague Island
August—Natural Chimneys Jousting Tournament, Harrisonburg
August—Virginia Highlands Arts and Crafts Festival, Abingdon
August—Old Fiddlers' Convention, Galax
September-October—Virginia Steeplechase Race Meet, Middleburg
September-October—National Beagle Trials, Middleburg
October—National Tobacco Festival, Richmond
October—Harvest Bowl, Roanoke
October—Virginia State Fair, Richmond
October—Dog Mart, Fredericksburg
October—Antique Show, Virginia Beach
October—Autumn Pilgrimage, Richmond
October—Tobacco Festival, Abingdon
December-January—Christmas in Williamsburg

CAPITOL
DESIGNED BY JEFFERSON

INDEX

About the Author: Allan Carpenter was born in Waterloo, Iowa. He went to Iowa State College and then taught at a Des Moines Junior High School and at Drake University. He left teaching to found the magazine *Teachers' Digest* which he published for eight years. He has been associated with publishing for many years and now works full time as a freelance writer. His first book was published when he was twenty and since then he has written more than fifty books.

About the illustrator: Roger Herrington grew up in Sault Ste. Marie, Michigan, on the American side of the Soo Locks. His stepfather was a tugboat captain and the family traveled with him to many parts of the United States. While he was in college, Roger worked during summers as a boatman on the Erie Canal. He went to the American Academy of Art in Chicago for his art training, and spent two years at the Ringling School of Art in Sarasota, Florida. He now has his own studio in Chicago and devotes most of his time to illustrating books for young people.